The Sanctified Life

by

Beverly Carradine

First Fruits Press
Wilmore, Kentucky
c2015

The Sanctified Life, by Beverly Carradine

First Fruits Press, ©2015
Previously published by the Pentecostal Publishing Company, 1897.

ISBN: 9781621714385 (print), 9781621714392 (digital), 9781621714408 (kindle)

Digital version at http://place.asburyseminary.edu/firstfruitsheritagematerial/116/

First Fruits Press is a digital imprint of the Asbury Theological Seminary, B.L. Fisher Library. Asbury Theological Seminary is the legal owner of the material previously published by the Pentecostal Publishing Co. and reserves the right to release new editions of this material as well as new material produced by Asbury Theological Seminary. Its publications are available for noncommercial and educational uses, such as research, teaching and private study. First Fruits Press has licensed the digital version of this work under the Creative Commons Attribution Noncommercial 3.0 United States License. To view a copy of this license, visit http://creativecommons.org/licenses/by-nc/3.0/us/.

For all other uses, contact:

First Fruits Press
B.L. Fisher Library
Asbury Theological Seminary
204 N. Lexington Ave.
Wilmore, KY 40390
http://place.asburyseminary.edu/firstfruits

Carradine, Beverly, 1848-1931

   The Sanctified Life / by Beverly Carradine.
   286 pages : Portrait ; 21 cm.
   Wilmore, Ky. : First Fruits Press, © 2015.
   Reprint. Previously published: Louisville, KY: Pentecostal Publishing Company, © 1897.
   ISBN: 9781621714385 (pbk.)
   1. Sanctification. I. Title.
BT 765 .C34 2015   234.8

Cover design by Kelli Dierdorf

First Fruits Press
The Academic Open Press of Asbury Theological Seminary
204 N. Lexington Ave., Wilmore, KY 40390
859-858-2236
first.fruits@asburyseminary.edu
asbury.to/firstfruits

REV. B. CARRADINE.

THE SANCTIFIED LIFE

BY

REV. B. CARRADINE, D. D.,

AUTHOR OF "SANCTIFICATION," "A JOURNEY TO PALESTINE," "THE LOTTERY EXPOSED," "CHURCH ENTERTAINMENTS," "THE BOTTLE," "SECRET SOCIETIES," "THE SECOND BLESSING IN SYMBOL," "THE BETTER WAY," "THE OLD MAN," "PASTORAL SKETCHES AND REVIVAL SERMONS."

PENTECOSTAL PUBLISHING CO.,

LOUISVILLE, KY.

1897.

Copyrighted, 1897, M. W. Knapp.

CONTENTS.

CHAPTER I.
Different Theories in Regard to Sanctification or Heart Purity 5

CHAPTER II.
The True Theory 17

CHAPTER III.
The Blessing is Obtainable Now 29

CHAPTER IV.
The Blessing May be Lost 40

CHAPTER V.
The Blessing Can be Recovered 54

CHAPTER VI.
How to Keep The Blessing 64

CHAPTER VII.
Some Features of The Sanctified Life 77

CHAPTER VIII.
The Loneliness of The Life 89

CHAPTER IX.
Prayer and Reading 106

CHAPTER X.
Witnessing 119

CHAPTER XI.
Good Works 139

CONTENTS.

CHAPTER XII.
FASTING, TITHES, AND DRESS.................................... 152

CHAPTER XIII.
MOODS, AFFINITIES, AND IMPRESSIONS..................... 167

CHAPTER XIV.
DOUBTS, FEARS, AND FRET...................................... 183

CHAPTER XV.
COME-OUT-ISM AND PUT-OUT-ISM............................ 200

CHAPTER XVI.
SECRET SOCIETIES... 220

CHAPTER XVII.
SIDETRACKS... 236

CHAPTER XVIII.
THE GREAT REMEDY.. 267

THE SANCTIFIED LIFE.

CHAPTER I.

DIFFERENT THEORIES IN REGARD TO SANCTIFICATION, OR HEART PURITY.

THE Saviour in His Sermon on the Mount said: "Blessed are the pure in heart." Can any one believe that Christ would bless a class of people who do not or can not exist? If men so insist, then do they make the Saviour utter an absurdity.

Regeneration implanted spiritual life in the soul, cleansed the nature from personal sin and guilt, gave a title to Heaven and communicated power over the world, the flesh and the devil; but neither the Bible or experience say it made us holy. It is a pity that some people do not study the meaning of the word regenerate. The trouble to-day is that it is loaded down with definitions that do not belong to the word; for some have made it mean anything and everything in order to leave no room for a second work of grace.

It is well to remember that a new heart is one thing, and a pure heart another. They are not synonymous. A man can have a new heart which loves God, and yet not possess a pure heart from which self, man-fear, love of praise and other like things are banished. The new heart comes with regeneration, the pure heart by the Baptism of the Holy Ghost and of fire. We are born unto one and baptized into the other. Born of water and the Spirit, but baptized with the Holy Ghost and with fire.

All churches agree that heart purity or sanctification is to be possessed. They only differ as to the time in which it may be obtained, and as to the agency or power through which it is effected. But this is a very great difference, and of gravest moment to the soul seeking to be holy. We call attention to some of these views.

One is the Purgatorial Theory. This, as is well known, is held by the Roman Catholic Church. They believe in pardon here in time, but that purification is obtained by flames burning in a kind of middle world, which they call Purgatory. The objection to this theory is that the Bible does not teach it, and there are some of us who want a "thus saith the Lord" on so vital a matter. An additional objection to this teaching is that it ascribes to a material flame what should be accomplished by the blood of Jesus Christ. There goes up a protest from the heart as we see the crown which belongs to the Son of God placed upon a bit of fire, and a marvelous work of grace which is attributed by the Bible to Him, ascribed to a flame, which we know to be an unintelligent and unspiritual agency.

A second opinion held is the Death Theory. There are many who believe and insist that purity or holiness can only come to the soul in the moment of death. The serious objection to this view is that there is nothing in the Bible to give foundation for such a teaching. Moreover this idea of death purification springs from the old false notion that sin is in matter. This position has long ago been made untenable. The absurdity of saying that sin is in a non-intelligent substance must at once strike the reader. So we conclude that sin is not to be found in wood, leather, cloth, skin, bone, muscle, or any other form of matter. It must and can only exist in spirit. The view, therefore, that located sin in the material nature of man, failed to see that the body was simply an unconscious instrument of the soul within; and supposing that the word "flesh" in the Bible meant the body, they fell upon the conclusion that the only hope of deliverance was by laying down the body in the grave.

An additional fault we find with this view is in its attributing purifying power to Death. Death is not an entity, but simply a dissolution of soul and body. There is nothing in the parting of the two natures to produce holiness. Moreover, if Death purifies or sanctifies then is it a saviour. Indeed, it does what Christ has not been able to do, according to these false notions. He could pardon, but Death they say purifies! Nor is this all of the absurdity of this view; for if Death purifies us, then is Death a friend! But the Bible distinctly says that Death is an enemy; "the last enemy that shall be destroyed is death."

We can not but offer the following thought to all who believe that we are only made pure and holy in death; that if this be so, then it is a great pity for people to get well who are sick. All drug stores should be discontinued, and physicians should be remonstrated with who are trying to restore indisposed and diseased people to health and life. They should be told that they are making a great mistake. "Do you not know, Doctor," we should say to them, "that if you let this man die he will become pure; but if you restore him, you are simply helping to protract and prolong sin in him and in his life?" The utter untenableness of the idea is seen without our adding another argument.

A third view is the Reformation Theory. Those who hold to this simply bid men to quit their badness. The exhortation is to stop doing wrong, join the church, lead a moral life, and the first thing they know they will be clean and pure.

This is the world's idea of holiness. It makes a man his own saviour, and as a moral procedure is nothing but whitewashing. The trouble with whitewash is that it comes off in a driving rain or through the course of time. The fence has not been changed, but simply coated. The old rotten plank is still underneath. We want something better than this in religion. It is not a coat of paint we want, but a new fence, not to be whitewashed, but washed white. The world white washes, but Jesus washes white. We read once of an old inn in England called The Inn of the Black Dragon. A gentleman bought it, and not liking the sign painted it out, and on the new coat had the picture of a white lamb drawn. The hotel was now The Inn of the White Lamb. And so the sign creaked in the breezes for several years, pelted by the snow and rain and rocked by the wind. One night there was a fearful storm, and next morning the landlord, on walking out on the pavement, glanced upward at his sign, and lo! the lamb was gone, and there pawing in the air was the old black dragon. The last storm of rain had washed off the lamb.

Herein is seen the trouble with the Reformation business. It is a skin-deep matter. It is manners rather than morals. It is a superficial coat instead of a radical change, and any time under a severe provocation the lamb is likely to disappear and the dragon take the deck.

We once saw when a lad a piece of candy with the word LOVE appearing in red color on the end of the stick. On biting off an end of it, the word was still seen. Deeper down we went in saccharine bites, but the word LOVE was always there. In fact, it ran through the whole stick. This is the way we want cleansing. We desire it through and through. No matter how deep men may go in their investigation, nor how knives may chop us off here and there, yet, recognized by men and felt by ourselves, we want the purifying work of Christ to abide.

A fourth view is the Zinzendorfian Theory. This teaching affirms that purity is obtained in regeneration. Concerning this false piece of theology, Mr. Wesley said that such a doctrine had never been heard of until Zinzendorf, a German Count, arose to teach it. It is well known how he wrote and preached against the heresy.

Truly, it seems that Methodism has drifted marvelously when her preachers can turn against the well-known declarations of her founder, and proclaim the opinions of a German Count as Methodist truth, when Mr. Wesley opposed and denounced it wherever he went. William Bramwell declared that he foresaw this doctrine would be the devil's big gun; and so it has proved. The amazing subtilty as well as fatality of this movement of Satan is seen at once when we call attention to the fact that he secures the same end by this teaching that he did when he had men believing for ages that they could never be made pure and be saved from sin in this world. As light poured in on men's minds through the pages of Holy Writ, and they saw that holiness was promised and possible, the great Adversary changed his tactics and taught that heart purity or holiness is obtained in regeneration. The astonishing fact is that by two such different teachings the same result is achieved—sin is left in the heart. For if men are taught that they have all in regeneration, the "pressing after," the "groaning for" the full deliverance does not take place, and so inbred sin is left unpurged in the soul.

As we stated in a chapter in "The Old Man," if regeneration is purity, then the advocates of this doctrine should have the following proofs: They should have analogies of nature teaching perfection in birth; the statement of God's Word declaring regenerated people to be pure; and the testimony of God's children saying that they have so found it in their experience. But when we come to look for these evidences, there is not one to be found. As for the analogies in nature, while we have abundance to prove perfection in creation, there are none to teach perfection or cleanness in birth. Nothing is born physically perfect in the animal kingdom, whether among beasts or men. A faithful examination will prove this. As for the Bible, it distinctly recognizes and names a principle or nature of evil left in the child of God. In one place it is called a "filthiness of spirit"; and any one can see that this could not be a material something. As for Christian testimony, we find that while men will insist in controversial articles, hundreds of miles away, that they obtained all in regeneration, yet when it comes to standing up in a testimony meeting where many eyes are upon them, and above all God is felt to be searchingly and powerfully present, that at such times and places they are most significantly silent. In addition to all this is the voiceless but strong opinion of the families and friends of these brethren that they did not "get it all" at conversion, that regeneration, whatever else it may have accomplished, had not made them pure.

The fifth view is the Growth Theory. Many thousands hold to this in all the different churches. Their position is that pardon and spiritual life are realized in regeneration, but holiness or entire sanctification comes as a development. It is away over yonder in the future somewhere. It is dim from its great distance from us. If we attain at all, it must be by the long process of a silent growth. This method, among other excellencies, disturbs no one's sensibilities by the noise of a sudden arrival. In the concern for the feelings of certain people, it looks like they do not propose to arrive at all.

The mistake that these brethren make is in confounding purity and maturity. Maturity or mellowness or ripeness comes with the flight of time, both in nature and grace, but the blessing we are contending for is not maturity but purity—a grace that is to be obtained as suddenly and sensibly as pardon.

Moreover, the people of God who hold to the growth view are confronted with the embarrassing fact that they can not present a single instance of a Christian coming into this blessing by development. This embarrassment is manifest when asked to produce a witness. They can not do it. Such a person has never and will never be found. Repeatedly the author has asked the question of large congregations in all parts of the United States, that he might establish by the answer the real truth, and he has never yet found a single person who received it by growth. On the contrary, many thousands have stood on their feet to witness that they obtained the grace instantaneously by an act of faith in Christ.

We can not but affirm that if a man had been traveling on a train from St. Louis to Cincinnati for a week, and had not reached his destination, that there would be reason to believe he was on the wrong road. But what if he had been going a year!—and what if he had been traveling twenty or thirty years, yes, forty years, and still had not reached Cincinnati! Then he ought to know he was on the wrong road, and the most sensible thing to do would be to change cars, conductors, tickets, direction and everything. Not less true is it that if a person has been seeking for sanctification along the Christian growth line for ten, twenty or forty years, and has not yet obtained the rich grace, that here is unmistakable evidence that he is on the wrong route. It would be wisdom indeed to look in the Word and see if there is not a speedier and truer way.

Of course, the advocates of the Growth Theory have Scriptures to quote to prove their view. One very popular verse is "grow in grace"! To which we reply, Certainly; but this does not say "grow *into* grace." There is a great difference between "grow in" and "grow into." No man can grow "into" a grace of God, but after being inducted by divine power, it is the most natural and easy thing for him after that to "grow *in* grace." A tree can not grow *into* another field, but if transplanted can easily then grow *in* it. So a sinner can not grow into repentance. God's power puts him there, and being there, then he grows *in* grace. So a Christian can not grow into sanctification. Again the divine power is used to place him in the new experience, but once in, then he can grow in grace. Again, no saint can grow into heaven. Here God lifts him the third time and plants him in the fields of life. Immediately he begins to grow in grace in heaven. So we grow in grace in regeneration, sanctification, and heaven; but we could not and did not grow into a single one of them.

There are other Scripture passages which they quote,

but as we have answered them in "The Old Man" we will not repeat here.

Again, there is the Imputation Theory. This is held by a number of excellent people. They say that the heart is never made entirely clean in this life, but purity is imputed to it through Christ. One of these advocates was talking with a Bishop in the M E. Church, and in the course of the conversation said: "My heart is dark and foul; I find corruption in it. But Jesus comes and throws His white robe of purity over my black heart, and no one can see the blackness. And when Christ appears for His own He will come to me as I am thus covered up, and will take me off with His robe." The Bishop meditated a moment and said: "Yes; Christ is coming for His own one of these days; and when He arrives He will do this very thing. But the black and foul do not belong to Him, so He will take His robe and leave you."

Imputed purity will not do. We want something deeper and more subjective. We know what imputed purity in a legal sense in the Bible means; but that same Bible teaches that we are brought into heaven not simply in a legal way, but are fitted for it as well. It is not only an imputed purity, but an *imparted* purity. The Word says: "From all *your* filthiness will I cleanse you"—"I will purge away thy dross and take away thy tin." This is what God promises and what the soul craves and must have to see God.

"What is imputed purity," said a man once, "but a snowstorm in a barnyard?" "Yes," replied a Salvation Army Captain, "and what if there should be a thaw!"

The trouble is that the "thaw" does come in such cases, and then what a moral, or rather immoral, spectacle we behold!

Let men deny and argue as they will, the yearning for a pure heart is left in the regenerate soul, and it is a longing not for something imputed to it in a hazy kind of way, but something given and enjoyed as a blessed, blissful possession. Moreover, the fact that this longing is in the regenerated heart shows that it is a grace as yet unpossessed, and so should inspire and urge the believer on unweariedly until he comes into the realization of the crowning blessing of the Christian life.

CHAPTER II.

THE TRUE THEORY.

THE true theory of entire sanctification is that it is an instantaneous work of God wrought in the soul of a regenerated man or woman in answer to perfect consecration, unswerving faith, and importunate prayer.

That there is a growth in grace before the reception of this blessing, and a rapid growth afterwards, is hereby affirmed, and no intelligent teacher of holiness thinks of denying. But neither the ante growth or the post growth is the work itself of which we speak. That work, which cleanses the heart from *all* sin, no matter how preceded by mortification of spirit and crucifying of the flesh, is done in a moment, in the twinkling of an eye, by the mighty power of God.

We are never to confound the things we do with what God does. We get ready for Him. We place ourselves in position, and the fire descends. We sanctify ourselves that He might sanctify us.

It is God's work. The Bible abounds in such statements. "Create in me a clean heart, O God." "He will purify the sons of Levi." "From all your filthiness and all your idols will I cleanse you."

"Christ loved the church and gave himself for it, that he might sanctify and cleanse it with the washing of water by the word, that he might present it to himself a glorious church, not having spot or wrinkle or any such thing; but that it should be holy and without blemish."

This purification is never attributed as a result to death or growth in grace, but is always declared to be the work of God.

It is therefore quite astonishing when we declare the fact of God's cleansing the heart from all remaining sin that men should call it "our theory." It is not our teaching, but the Bible's own statement. It is impossible to read the Word without seeing it everywhere.

It is wonderful how the plain setting forth of God's Word is called a "theory," and so branded and avoided. A presiding elder was speaking to a sanctified preacher on his district, and said: "I recognize your lovely spirit, excellent life and faithful ministry, but I can not endorse your theory." The preacher replied: "Well, here is a remarkable thing. Suppose I am presented with an apple which is large and rosy, has a pleasant smell and delicious taste; and I say to it, Apple, you are large, rosy, fragrant and luscious, but I can not endorse the tree that grew you. Now, brother, this speech would not be more surprising and unreasonable on my part than yours to me; for you admit that my spirit and life are all right and gospel labors successful, and yet refuse to endorse the very blessing by which I obtained this spirit and achieve this success."

It is nothing on earth but the opposition of the carnal mind to the divine way of doing things. This is God's method of purifying the heart. He does it Himself. In like manner men resisted the faith theory of justification in Luther's time, and so men oppose the faith theory of an instantaneous sanctification to-day. But it will yet be seen on earth, as it will be perfectly known in heaven, that the "Second Blessing Theory," so often ridiculed and assailed, is God's way of sanctifying the soul. The ridicule hurled at it is no indication of its not being true, for it stands in good company in the matter of an undeserved obloquy. So the multitude jeered at Christ on the cross. So men laugh at the Bible, and at the doctrines of the Resurrection and the Final Judgment. And so have I seen them laugh at revival meetings when the Holy Ghost was saving people and they were shouting the praises of God. Men mocked at Pentecost, and continue to ridicule the truth and work of God. A minister said in the preachers' meeting of a large Western city that "he was convinced that the whole second blessing movement was born in hell." There was not a preacher present who enjoyed the blessing of sanctification. Most of them were skeptical in regard to the matter, and were trying to keep it out of their churches; but at this fearful remark there was a chorus of protesting voices from the entire body: "No, no, brother; don't say that!" The speech of the excited man bordered wonderfully near to blasphemy against the Holy Ghost. To say that the holiness movement, inspired and swept onward by the Holy Spirit, is a work born in hell is frightfully similar to the utterance of the angry Jews when Christ by the power of the Spirit cast out devils in their presence. They said He did it by the power of Beelzebub, locating the power and origin of the miracle in hell. It, was then Jesus turned and said: "The blasphemy against the Holy Ghost shall not be forgiven." This He said, Mark writes, "because they said He had an unclean spirit." They gave a divine work a hellish origin.

But no matter how men deny and resist, the Bible teaches that the purification of the heart is the work of God. Peter tells how this purifying came by faith on the day of Pentecost, and John states that it is while "we walk in the light," "having fellowship one with another," that then "the blood of Jesus Christ cleanseth us from all sin." As thus taught in God's Word, it is a divine work and subsequent to regeneration. Mr. Wesley says the last quoted verse is one of the strongest passages to teach the second work. Of course, the word "cleanseth" is in the present tense, and this very fact gives the idea of the constant, unbroken, perpetual sense of cleanness that comes with the blessing of entire sanctification. But not less clear is the truth that this cleansing from *all* sin came while the man was "*in the light*" and enjoying Christian "*fellowship.*"

But, says an objector, I do not believe that God has to do His work over again. The answer to this is that sanctification is not the doing over of regeneration, but is a different work altogether. The second work being not to improve regeneration but to eliminate inbred sin.

Still, with this explanation, the objector has spoken hastily in saying God does not have to do his work over again. This He certainly does in the recovery of every backslider.

But, says the objector again, I do not believe that God does a second work; I believe He accomplishes everything He has to do in one work.

The reply to this is that, plausible as is the speech, everything contradicts it in nature and grace. The first contradiction is from the world, which as it rolls through space says God made me by six distinct touches or works; every one was different, and all six together made me the habitable earth I am to-day.

The second contradiction comes from the human family. When Adam was created, the race in its federal nature was not completed. It takes not only male but female to make man, and the two were not made at once. God first created man and then afterwards made the woman and brought her to Adam. There are few but will admit that the second work was an improvement on the first. So it took two works to make what is properly called man. The author can not see how a woman can get her consent to fight the second blessing when she is a second blessing herself.

The third contradiction is seen in the two covenants God has at different times given the world. The Bible says there were two, and Paul distinctly says that the first was not perfect. Some people insist that every one of God's works is perfect; they seem to know more than the Lord Himself, for He affirms in His own Word that the first covenant was not faultless, while in James we read that "every good gift and every perfect gift is from above," showing that there is a difference in God's gifts, some being good and some perfect. Regeneration is never called perfection in the Bible; but being regenerated, we are told to go on to perfection. So the first covenant not being faultless, God gives another that is perfect, in which the "old sin is purged"; there is no more "remembrance of sin," and the worshiper himself is "made perfect." Two works are beheld in regard to the covenants.

The fourth contradiction to the statement that God does everything in one work is seen in what took place with the disciples on the day of Pentecost. They evidently received a new divine work or grace on the morning of the tenth day. That they were converted men and women when they went into the upper room there can be no doubt if language means anything. Christ said they were branches of the true Vine, that their names were in the Book of Life, and that they were not of the world, even as He was not of the world. He had sent them forth to preach the Gospel, and this He has never done with sinners. They had cast out devils, and Christ said that a devil could not cast out a devil, else was the house of Satan divided. In addition to all this, days before He had breathed upon them and said: "Receive ye the Holy Ghost." Who can read these statements and descriptions and not see that they were saved men and women? Yet on the morning of the tenth day suddenly the power of God fell upon them and they were all filled with the Holy Ghost, and they began to speak with new tongues. Peter leaped to his feet and cried out: "This is what Joel said should take place in the last days." This one speech of Peter proves it was a new grace or blessing received. Here was something long ago prophesied just sent down upon them. Certainly this could not be pardon and regeneration, for men had enjoyed the justified experience all along. Surely the patriarchs, prophets, David, Simeon, Anna, and John the Baptist had religion. The very astonishment and gladness of the disciples showed that the blessing was new. Suppose, for instance, one of us should promise our children a remarkable breakfast. They could scarcely sleep for thinking what it would be, but of course looked for dainties and luxuries. But next morning, on filing into the dining room, they discovered the same old breakfast of bread, meat and coffee. One thing is certain, they would not be in a rapture, and none of them would spring on a chair and cry out in enthusiasm: "This is what Joel said should take place." If what happened at Pentecost was what had been experienced before, how can the joy and astonishment and quotation of Peter be reconciled with the facts? No! instead of this we are brought face to face again with the second work of grace. The marvelous change that took place in the disciples from this hour settles the fact that it was a second work, not of pardon and life, but of purity and power.

The fifth contradiction is seen in what took place with the Saviour on the banks of Jordan when He was baptized with the Holy Ghost. All of us know that Christ was without sin, that Satan could find nothing in Him in all His beautiful and holy life; and yet on the banks of Jordan He received what had not come upon Him before, in the anointing or Baptism of the Holy Ghost. There are two works accomplished in the Baptism of the Holy Ghost as received by the Christian believer—"purifying the heart" and "enduement of power." In Christ's case, there was no inbred sin or moral taint of any kind to be purged away. All that could take place with His spotless human nature was the empowering of the Spirit. Hence the Holy Ghost did not descend on Him with fire, as in the case of the disciples, but as a dove. That the Saviour did receive the enduement of power then, is seen by the clear statements of Scripture. It was after this memorable morning that it is said that "He went forth in the *power* of the Spirit." This was not said of Him before. We are also made to remark the effect of this anointing immediately upon His ministry. We read that He went up to Nazareth and on the Sabbath day entered into the synagogue, and when the roll of Scripture was put in His hands He stood up to read, and selected as His text from Isaiah the very thing that had happened to Him on the River Jordan: "The Spirit of the Lord God is upon me: because he hath anointed me to preach good tidings unto the meek; he hath sent me to bind up the broken-hearted, to proclaim liberty to the captives and the opening of the prison to them that are bound; to proclaim the acceptable year of the Lord," etc. We read that He then sat down and began to preach, and all marveled at His words. Moreover, the discourse was so heart-searching and incisive that the officials of the synagogue became enraged and took hold of Him violently and tried to hurl Him down a precipice. Now lest any one should think this was Christ's first public talk or sermon, the Scripture says

He stood up that day in the synagogue "*according to His custom.*" The difference was that He had received the anointing of the Holy Ghost, and His words, now power-freighted, were simply overwhelming. It does seem to us that, in view of this occurrence, men should be slow in saying God does everything in one work. He does not. He did not even do so with His own Son. And when we hear a man say that he obtained all in repentance, and then note the one absolutely perfect man who ever lived receiving on the banks of Jordan the anointing or Baptism of the Holy Ghost, we are made to marvel at some people's mental density or spiritual arrogance.

The sixth contradiction is to be found in the two touches laid by the hand of Christ on the eyes of the blind man. It does seem to the writer that this second touch was given by the Saviour, if for no other reason than to close the mouths of people who say that God does everything in one work. Vision came with the first touch and perfect vision with the second. This very order ought to prepare the people to see how that love comes with one operation of divine grace and perfect love with another.

The seventh contradiction is seen in the word Redemption. Usually men think that the word stands for one work, when it really covers four. The first work wrought in the salvation of a soul is conviction. This can never be done by a man. It is a divine work.

It takes the Holy Ghost to burden a man for his sins, and when it is done that man is miserable and restless, and oftentimes can neither eat nor sleep. Still the man is not saved; he is simply convicted. But when he repents and believes on the Lord Jesus Christ the Holy Ghost works again and this time regenerates him. Still there is a third work, for Paul writes to regenerated people, and says, "This is the will of God even your sanctification," and still again, "The God of peace sanctify you wholly." He who regenerates can sanctify us wholly. But there is yet a fourth divine work, and this time upon the body. It is called the resurrection. The body is a part of man and is included in redemption. It is to be raised from the dust and out of death, and renewed with transcendent glory. This is the last work. Redemption is then completed. Instead, then, of one work, redemption includes four!—conviction, regeneration, entire sanctification, and resurrection. And yet there are some people who say that God does everything in one work.

Thus we meet the objections that God never has to do His work over again, and never does but one work. The sweeping away of these opposing thoughts leaves us with the blessed truth that God can and will and does purify the pardoned soul. It is His work and our privilege.

Thank God that when Christ came to this world

He did not appear in our midst with one gift of grace, but with two. He had no empty hand, but both were full for the human family—Pardon in one for the sinner, and Purity in the other for the believer. May every child of God lose no more time, but press forward at once and receive the blessing that has been long waiting him

CHAPTER III.

THE BLESSING IS OBTAINABLE NOW.

IF God can purify the heart and will not, He would be a strange God. There would be room here for the charge of divine indifference and even cruelty, if this was so.

If the Divine Being would purify the soul and can not, then we have a weak and helpless Lord to worship. But who will say for a moment that He can not? And who would believe that He will not?

The fact is that God is able and willing to sanctify the soul. If able and willing to do it, there certainly is no need of postponing the work to the hour of death. To thus remand our expectation to the very brink of the grave is to reflect on the goodness as well as holiness of the Almighty. We can not afford to do this.

Certainly if God is willing to do the work, and He alone can do it, why should we not seek it now, and expect and receive it now?

The blessing of sanctification is taught in one place as a purifying of the heart and an empowering for service. In another place it is described as the entrance of Christ into the soul as an indweller. The same truth is taught under this change of terms, for the Lord will not abide unbrokenly in the heart until inbred sin is cleansed away by the Baptism of the Holy Ghost and fire, and the result of that constant indwelling is bound to be power. So "purifying" and "empowering" is the same thing as Christ's entrance into the soul to abide permanently. It was this He referred to in the fourteenth chapter of John when He said: "We will come unto him and make our abode with him." When this takes place, the man will find that he has purity and power; in a word, sanctified.

How may such a wonderful blessing be obtained? Let us see if we can not present the matter in such a way that the hungry, watchful soul can go right into this beautiful grace of God.

One of the frequent descriptions given of man in the Bible is that of a house, building or temple. "Ye are God's building," says the apostle; and again, "Know ye not that ye are the temple of God?"

We were originally made or built for God to dwell in. Satan marred the plan of Heaven by taking possession of us. Some of you have seen a beautiful dwelling pass out of the hands of the first owners and finally become the abode of poverty and degradation. The writer once looked at a famous hotel that in its palmy days had seen in its spacious rooms and halls the beauty, chivalry and statesmanship of a large Southern State. But at the time he viewed it, about the only thing left of the magnificence was its colossal size. It had become a tenement for the vilest and most poverty-stricken classes in the city. The paint had faded from the wall, doors were gone or hanging on a single hinge, and window panes were broken and stuffed with rags. Dark-looking dissipated and ragged figures lounged about the portals or hung out of the windows; dogs and pigs roamed unchecked through the lower halls and galleries; and one could scarcely realize that this place had once been as attractive as it was now revolting

So Satan took God's building and rubbed off the colors of grace and innocence, planted decay and moral ugliness where he could, filled the door of the mouth with all kinds of uncleanness, hung forbidding looks out of the windows of the eyes, and shocked the beholder in every way. But through grace this house is redeemed from the devil. It becomes the Lord's again. It is washed, cleansed, and warmed, and recognized as God's property. Everybody marks the delightful change.

There is one thing, however, that constitutes a painful experience to the redeemed man himself, and which is evident as a fact to the observer, and that is the Saviour is not an abider in this house which belongs to Him. He is a visitor, coming and going, but not a steady, constant indweller.

This visiting Christ, now consciously in the soul and

now as consciously absent, will upon compliance with conditions on our part come into us and take up His fixed and unchanging abode. When this happens, sanctification happens. The purifying Spirit goes through the soul, and Christ enters to leave no more if we will have it so.

How is this entering in and blessed possession of us to take place? The whole matter is made clear by following out a line of thought suggested by the image or figure of the building. Remember that the Saviour's word is that if we will do certain things, "we will come unto Him and make our abode with Him." And remember that visiting is one thing and abiding is another. Some of you will recall the first time you ever saw your wife. She was paying a visit at your father's home. It was a brief call, but it affected you forever and changed the house itself. The room she stood in looked different, the furniture assumed a new and peculiar luster, the goblet out of which she drank water you quietly set aside as your own, determining that no other lips should desecrate it. The old brick walk down which she went, and the gate with its overarching trees through which she passed, took upon themselves a subtle charm and glory. This was only a visit, but a year from that time she came again, and this time to stay. She came with trunks and baggage and took up her abode. She was now your wife.

The blessing we speak of changes Christ from a visitor to an abider in the heart. His visits were beautiful and blessed, but alas for the absences! How we used to sing:

"Return, O Holy Dove, return,"

and

"How tedious and tasteless the hours
When Jesus no longer I see."

The indwelling is what we want; Christ to move in, take possession and never leave us any more.

This is brought about by a method analagous to what we see when a person moves into an earthly home.

First, the house is to be emptied. If a man purchases a building from you, there is one thing he expects, and that you do,—you empty it for him. He does not want your old goods and chattels. He has furniture of his own, and doubtless much better than the kind you possess. So in offering yourself as the Lord's dwelling place, He demands that you let everything go, keep nothing back, and, in a word, empty yourself.

This is only another way of describing consecration. A man who is laying everything on the altar is simply emptying himself. As the consecration proceeds, the person is conscious of an increasing emptiness, and just before the blessing comes, in describing his experience he would say: I have given up everything, am all emptied, and have nothing as yet in return except the conviction that I have done right.

The writer illustrated this emptying process in his church in St. Louis. In front of the pulpit stretched a large altar in the form of a semi-circle. Its shape was made to stand for the heart. At the beginning of the illustration there were a number of persons in the altar, besides books, papers, overcoats, hats, etc., etc. The preacher quietly put the individuals out and off the platform, saying that he would not let a single human being fill the place where Christ should reign. After this he threw out the hats, overcoats, gloves and wraps, declaring that the dress question should be settled in that manner. Then he removed the handsome chairs from the stand, affirming that rich furniture should not be an idol with him. Then he picked up some books and papers and put them outside the altar, with the remark that men's writings and opinions should not stand a moment before the known will and command of God. About this time the altar looked exceedingly empty; but still the illustrator was not satisfied. Going about, he found minute things, like bits of paper and thread on the floor. Stooping down, he carefully picked them up and cast them outside the altar rail saying: "Nothing, no matter how small, shall stay." At last only himself and the Bible were left inside the altar-heart. Whereupon, after placing the Holy Book in the very center of the altar, he himself stepped out, declaring as he went that the Word of God should alone rule and reign in that heart.

A hundred or more people stood around looking at this figurative sermon. There was not an individual who looked into the emptied, silent altar, with the solitary Bible in the center of the platform, but felt solemnized, and grasped with a convicting clearness what emptying of the heart meant and must be in order that Christ might come.

This is unquestionably the hard thing with many to do. Yet it must be done. It may take days, but there will be no divine incoming until there is the human emptying. How is it possible to fill us until we are first emptied? How could God truthfully say we had His fullness when something of self and the world was left? Emptied first, filled afterward is the order. The disciples were ten days engaged in the human part of the work. We once thought they were ten days getting filled with the Holy Ghost, but they were ten days getting emptied. It does not take God ten seconds to fill thoroughly and overflowingly the self-emptied man. God moves at once into the vacated dwelling.

Second, the house must be cleansed. That individual would be lacking in self-respect who would turn an untidy and defiled building over to the man who had purchased and desired to move into it.

So there is a cleansing of hands and hearts to

obtain Jesus, the indwelling Sanctifier, in our souls. There was a cleansing in regeneration from all personal guilt and sin. Yet is there a deeper purifying for the man in whom the Son of God will abide forever. The disciples, in the sixteenth chapter of John, were called "clean" by Christ, but in the seventeenth chapter He prayed His Father to "sanctify" them, and sanctify means to make pure and holy. To obtain this profounder purification which removes the principle itself of sin, we are called upon to cleanse ourselves first. This does not mean that the regenerated man is a sinner. What is meant will be taught him in that hour when he pants for Jesus to come into him.

Sanctify yourselves; for the Lord your God will sanctify you. There is a double sanctification, a human and a divine. We sanctify and then God sanctifies. We cleanse the life and He cleanses the soul. We attend to the seen and He to the unseen.

A woman will wash the windows and floors of the house for the new owner, but we never yet knew the incoming female satisfied with the washing or house cleansing of the outgoing woman. She at once travels over the track of her scouring predecessor with soap, brush and broom, giving what she calls a better cleaning. So in like manner, deep as may be our purifying, God purifies still deeper. We may brush down the spider webs, but it takes the Lord to kill the spider.

Third, you must stand at the door of an emptied

and cleansed house and watch and wait for the coming of the owner. This is what we have seen people do. The house had been prepared and the former possessor stood with keys in hand awaiting the arrival of the new purchaser.

So should the seeker of sanctification stand at the door of his own emptied heart and look up for his descending Lord. We never knew of Christ coming with this blessing to any other than to such an upward looker and expecter. As the writer recalls certain ones he has seen sanctified, his heart melts and eyes fill from the bare memory as he sees them again with that indescribably pathetic gaze, the soul in the eyes, looking and longing for Jesus to descend and fill His blood-bought home.

Of course, we do not mean that the physical glance is always upward. Sometimes it is not and the head is bowed, but the soul-gaze is always heavenward, no matter where the bodily eyes may be resting. Moreover, we all recognize the fact of this spiritual uplook and feel at the same time that something will soon happen to the wistful gazer, and it does.

Happy the man who will not allow himself to be diverted and distracted, but having emptied and cleansed his heart, will stand waiting with ardent prayer and expectation for Christ to descend, fill, and ever after remain as the glorious indweller of the soul.

It is the attitude of surrender and devotement,

the spirit of faith and the grace of supplication all united in one person. Such an one will not be disappointed. Christ is certain to come. He can not stay away.

At this juncture comes the filling, or taking possession. Just as an earthly owner sweeping up with carriages and vans moves into his new home, so Jesus descends in chariots of fire with the furniture of heaven to fill and take possession of the perfectly consecrated and waiting soul. What an epoch, and what an experience! Who can forget it? The very memory arising in after years fills the eyes and sets the soul on fire anew.

> 'Jesus comes. He fills my soul,
>   Perfected in love I am;
> I am every whit made whole,
>   Glory, glory to the Lamb."

Or, as sung by Charles Wesley over one hundred years ago:

> "He visits now the house of clay;
>   He shakes His future home;
> O wouldst thou, Lord, in this glad day
>   Into thy temple come.
>
> "Come, O my God, thyself reveal
>   Fill all this mighty void;
> Thou only canst my spirit fill;
>   Come, O my God, my God."

We recall a lady who the morning she received this blessing was leaning against a great pillar in the center of the church. What a hungry, wistful look she had! Her hands were folded and eyes looking upward, when suddenly the glorious blessing came in the entrance of the Blesser. With a great rapturous cry that went through every heart she fell forward as if shot through the heart with a musket ball.

Another lady we remember who had consecrated believed, prayed, waited, looked and received Jesus into her soul in the sweetest, gentlest way. We saw her afterwards at the altar with an uplifted look, and perfectly abstracted from her surroundings. With a strange, sweet smile on the face, her eyes seemed fixed on worlds out of sight. For an hour she never moved a muscle nor closed an eyelid. People passed before her, but she seemed to look through them. It was like one hanging out of a window of Time, gazing into Eternity. She seemed to be looking at Christ and into heaven, while the soul's voiceless content and immeasurable calm was written in every line of the rapt countenance. No one was able to behold her without the tears gushing. All felt that Christ had come to His home and was abiding therein. A soul was hushed into perfect rest in the midst of a stormy world. The redeemed, encircled in the divine arms and pillowed on the divine breast, was looking into the face of the Redeemer.

> "Blessed quietness; holy quietness,
> What assurance fills my soul;
> On the stormy sea, Jesus speaks to me,
> And the billows cease to roll."

CHAPTER IV.

THE BLESSING MAY BE LOST.

WHEN one is told what sanctification is to the experience and life; what inward rest and outward activity, what usefulness and victory it brings, what deliverance from torment, and what mighty keeping power on the part of God is realized; the amazement is great that such a blessing should ever be lost.

For some reasons it is surprising. One would think that such a pearl of great price would be so jealously guarded that it could never be stolen. One would reason that such a life is so close to God, its joys so deep, its satisfaction so perfect, that scarcely anything on the outside could have sufficient force and influence to end so complete a union and so delightful an intimacy.

When, therefore, such cases are reported it causes some to doubt the fact that the fallen one ever had the grace. Others make it an argument and defense for the rejection of the blessing. In what respect, say they, is sanctification superior to regeneration if it can be lost.

The last point is plausible and is not without force

at the first hearing. But it falls to pieces, however, by the simple statement that our moral probation is not over at sanctification, and we may not only lose the grace of heart purity but the soul itself between the point of time called To-day and the Gates of Pearl.

There is much ignorance among many as to what is done in the work of sanctification. According to some, all possibility of sinning is removed. We are actually placed by such erroneous ideas above Adam, for he was in danger while in Eden, but these reasoners, or rather non-reasoners, would put an end to probation with us, make temptation a mere name and reduce the sanctified soul to the condition of a moral machine or automaton. Is it not surprising that they can not see the difference between an evil inclination and liability to sin? The power to sin is one thing, the proneness to do so is another. Sanctification takes out the latter, but leaves the former, which is an attribute or necessity in a free moral agent who is working out salvation. The proneness to sin may be removed, while the power to sin will remain until life is ended and we sweep into heaven, where we can not sin. So with this power angels fell somewhere in the skies. Adam fell in paradise, and regenerated and sanctified people can fall in this present world.

But while sanctification may be lost, yet it is unspeakably better while it is retained than the regenerated experience, as far as perfect love and peace tower above simple love and peace, and a great inward, steady, upwelling joy is more to be desired than one which is as variable as the winds and fluctuating as the tides.

The fact, however, remains that sanctification can be lost, and this is no more an argument against its truth and blessedness, than backsliding can be used to refute the doctrine and experience of justification.

The Bible in its warnings prepares us for this awful possibility. We are told to "watch" and "pray" and "strive," lest we fall into temptation. And as solemnly as a funeral bell falls the words, "Let him that thinketh he standeth take heed lest he fall." We are not only informed that Satan would deceive the very "elect," but we are shown him defiling the high priest Joshua and bringing down with an awful crash unto everlasting ruin one of the members of the Apostolic College whom Christ had chosen.

The ground and possibility of the fall of the sanctified is pictured in the house that had been swept and garnished, and yet Satan with other evil spirits returns to it and takes possession again, and the man's state, said Christ, "is worse than the first."

Again the Scriptural basis for such a fall is presented in the field of wheat in which there was not a single tare. Here is evidently a pure heart. But while the owner of the field slept an enemy came and sowed tares. The damage was done while the man slumbered. Herein is the explanation. We can by negligence, carelessness, sloth, lack of watchfulness allow the great adversary to resow his tares in our purified souls. If he did so in the clean spirit of Adam in Paradise, he can do so in the clean soul of a man in America. Satan does not resign his throne or give up his work because we get sanctified. If we become careless and sleepy he will sow the tares of inbred sin in us again.

After these pictures of the devil-repossessed house, and the field of wheat sown with tares, we are told in the Gospel of the denial of Peter, the fall of Judas, the ruin of Ananias, and the defection of Demas. Then follow the words of Paul: "I keep under my body and bring it into subjection; lest that by any means when I have preached to others I myself should be a castaway."

This is not all, nor the saddest nor darkest things that are to be found in the Scriptures in regard to the soul's downfall and destruction after having been in the highest states of grace.

The fact is we are free, and the soul feels it in every throb of its being. Each man is free, and life proves it, the world sees it, and the man knows it. With all the constraining and restraining grace of God, it is possible for man to break over every barrier and choose and secure his own downfall and ruin.

The testimony of a great number confirm the teaching of the Bible that this most beautiful and satisfying grace of God can be lost. Mr. Wesley even mentions the percentage of those who in different ways part with the blessing; a percentage, however, considerably less than the one he gives for those who lose justification. This is noteworthy, as it shows that sanctification is not only to be desired on account of its superior joys, but for the increased safety it brings.

Still it can be lost. We are to remember that Satan does not die because we get sanctified. Nor does he give a man up because he has a pure heart. If he assailed the innocent Adam in Eden, and the spotless Son of God on earth, he certainly will not pass by a sanctified soul without many and varied and violent assaults. He would particularly enjoy getting such a Son of Thunder once more in his power, locking again his formerly liberated lips, paralyzing his energies and drying up his glad and buoyant life.

There are many such shorn Samsons to-day in the land. Men who once towered in this grace and burned with holy fire. But they have been crippled in various ways, are sunk in gloom and silence, avoid the camp-meetings where holiness is sung, prayed, preached and shouted; while some have even gone over to the other side against us.

When men affect to wonder how a sanctified man can fall into sin, they not only overlook the facts we have mentioned concerning the free moral agency of man that can not be destroyed by any work of grace, but they fail to observe the route by which sin enters the soul. The knowledge of that alone as to how sin gets admission into the citadel of a man's life would explain the fall in the skies, the fall in Eden, and the fall of every being since that hour. Under this light it is seen that it does not require inbred sin to make a man transgress.

Sin to a free moral agent has to come first to the intellect. The thought or picture of the evil is presented. It is in the power of the man to immediately reject the thought and allow it no lodgment even for a moment. This is what should be done and is done by many. But if the conception, or picture, is allowed to remain in the mind, it passes at once into the region of the Sensibilities, and a commotion is felt within as a result. If still cherished, the realm of Desire is invaded and a longing for the forbidden thing is realized. The next strata of the moral nature that is now entered is the Will. The man determines upon the act of commission. Then after the determination of the Will the sin emerges into daylight in the form of an Act. Then follows repeated acts which result in Character, and Character settles the question of Destiny.

The route or descending stairway is seen at a glance in the following arrangement of the words:

>THOUGHT,
>DESIRE,
>WILL,
>ACT,
>HABIT,
>CHARACTER,
>DESTINY.

Here is a diagram proof showing that it is not necessary to have inbred sin in the heart in order to do wrong. The moral cognitions and the volitional powers of the man make an avenue for the entrance of evil just as they do for the admission of good. The blessing of sanctification, however, is not often lost through a flagrant sin or immorality. Satan would never come at first to the sanctified with gross temptations. He would at later periods of weakness, but at first he approaches in more subtle and refined methods in order to worm his way back into the heart from which he has been cast out.

The great majority of those who lose the blessing have done so from a failure in definite testimony. This appears strange to the opposers of sanctification who laugh derisively at such a blessing that is to be retained by a constant testifying to the fact of its presence and enjoyment. But they overlook the fact that the blessing is intended of God for all, and the testimony attracts attention, inflames desire for its possession, and so spreads the truth and increases the number of benefitted souls. Hence the silent possessor of holiness has committed a grave error. He has hidden his talent in a napkin, and the divine command now is, "Take it away from him." Mr. Fletcher lost the blessing four times because of his silence. He says so in the Life of Hester Ann Rogers. It is a false humility to be silent in regard to this grace, for it is not man's work we testify to, but God's. How many persons the writer has heard say in meetings all over the United States that through failure to testify they had lost the pearl of great price.

Again, the blessing may be lost by allowing the soul to become burdened again. Outward trials and troubles do not cease because the soul is baptized with the Holy Ghost. The disciples abounded in afflictions after their sanctification, although they also abounded in joy. Satan is very anxious to persuade the heart to accept the old load of mental care which Jesus took away in sanctification. Just a little fret and worry is injected, just a little repining and fault-finding, just a little self-pity and grief over our loneliness, lack of sympathy and peculiar life suffering, and so the wedge is driven in and the gap has commenced which, unless speedily closed, will result in the entire loss of the blessing. It is at the peril of losing the experience that the soul allows itself to criticize, repine, find fault and worry about anything. They that walk in the King's holy way must have pure hearts, gentle tongues, loving ways, happy faces and restful lives. There was once an old house in London that had a stone placed over its arched entrance which read: "No Burdens Allowed to Pass Here." This is the law of the sanctified life. To break it is to be shut out of the experience.

Again, the blessing may be lost by disobedience. One single act will hardly cause the whole gracious work of heart purity to be swept away unless it is a very grave transgression. But the smallest act of disobedience will bring shadows and loss of liberty, and if persisted in, is certain at last to bring a calamitous result.

The blessing of sanctification is lost gradually. It is a rare thing to see such a glorious light extinguished and life ended by a single deed. The rule is a slow leakage or gradual forfeiture. A very slight angle of divergence is formed, and by and by the fact of moral distance is not only felt by the drifting one, but is recognized by others.

There seems to be a certain order of departure with the blessing. First the joy goes. This is a tender, beautiful, upwelling gladness in the soul, and that never ceases if the man lives up to his privilege.

This is the crown and glory of sanctification. It is this which gives the bright look to the face, the flash to the eye, the bouyancy to the soul, and the inexpressible ring of gladness and triumph to the voice. This is the first thing that is affected when holiness, as an experience, begins to be lost.

We do not mean by this joy a feeling of ecstacy! We know people with this gladness who never have overwhelming transports and camp-meeting shouting experiences. But they possess the quiet inner joy born of conscious heart purity and the indwelling Christ, and that is read unmistakably in the happy smile, the deep, restful look in the eyes, and the unruffled peace that literally beams in the shining face. Nor do we mean that a temporary arrest of this joy signifies the fact of sin, or the loss of the blessing of sanctification. A short subsidence of this inner gladness may arise from causes not sinful. Mr. Wesley speaks of the joy being withheld for a little while, why it is done and what the person should do under the circumstances. Madame Guyon writes in one of her books that the withdrawal of joy at times is to wean us away from devotion to feelings. But as the joy we speak of is not an emotion like the camp-meeting blessing, but the soul's own gladness at being right and clean, we fail to agree with her.

It is the regular absence of this joy which should alarm us. The fact that it is received only for a few moments and then fades away rapidly, is the grave feature connected with its loss.

We once lost this joy for a few hours. It was not forfeited by a violation of any of the commandments. Nor was sanctification as a work of grace lost, but was felt to be still remaining. But the tender, beautiful, upwelling joy was gone which gave the glory, charm and power to sanctification. If we should live to be an hundred years old we will never forget the sharp distress of those hours. We were taught then by a negation and deprivation what sanctification was to the soul. With groans, sighs and tears we humbled ourselves before the Lord. We did not see how we could live without that joy, and what is more did not care to live without it. Suddenly it was restored, and as quietly as it had been taken away. With my face buried in my hands but covered with smiles, we knew the glory had come again. The sun was up, the springtime had come, and the watchman on the walls cried out as he walked, "All is well."

The second thing lost is liberty. The man finds himself hampered in different ways. The tongue grows stiff, and the presence of people begins to paralyze. The bird still sings, but with a feeling that it is in a cage. There is movement, but accompanied with a sensation of circumscribing bars and walls.

We do not speak here of a sense of mental and

physical heaviness that may arise from sickness, exhaustion and atmospheric conditions. This will necessarily happen to the best of people. We refer to the continued loss of true liberty that has for its cause something in the soul and life.

The third step in the departure of the blessing is the loss of power. It begins to dawn upon the individual that his words are not as effective as formerly; his prayers do not prevail; his testimonies fail to move and convince, or his preaching is resultless.

Here again we feel that we should spare the feelings of some truly sanctified people who are in difficult places and have little or no visible fruit and victories. It is well here to remember that Jesus Himself could do no mighty works in some places because of unbelief. Paul had a hard time at Athens, and there are families, churches, and communities to-day so set, crystallized and frozen that it will take the trumpet of the archangel Gabriel to arouse them.

Yet with these recognized difficulties, there is a conscious power granted the sanctified man even in the hardest of places. He feels that his words are energized, that they are not altogether lost, that God is not only with him, but standing by him and working through him. A man is as conscious of spiritual power as he is of physical strength. And that is not all, he is as conscious that this same spiritual force is gone as that physical energy has departed. He may articulate loudly, speak impressively, toss back the hair, look upward, wave the hand and bring it down with force, but he fails, and the people recognize that that indefinable something called unction or power is gone.

Finally, the blessing itself as a work of grace goes. We are not trying to split hairs in this description, but write what has been forced on our observation for years. We have seen men whose joy, liberty and power had gone, and yet they said they had something left which regeneration had never brought them. One would suppose that if joy, freedom and power had left the heart, all would be gone. But they insist that there is still something left, that they feel purity or cleanness and a certain rest or quiet of spirit. Granting that what they say is true, yet this itself will likewise go, and the man be left with nothing but the memory that he was once sanctified. Purity and rest are the two marked features of the blessing, and when they are gone the soul is bereft, and Ichabod is not only felt, but read in the life.

So it seems in God's mercy that the loss of the blessing is so marked by stages of decline, and declared by spiritual alarm bells, that any one can know what is going on, take the warning in time, fly to Christ and the cleansing blood, and so be prevented from the calamity of losing the greatest blessing that God has for the soul.

Certain it is that when lost, the soul is never happy again until it recovers it. There is nothing that can compensate for its loss.

Nothing can fill the heart once occupied by Jesus. All substitutes for the rest and joy which an indwelling Christ brought are felt to be utter failures. Sanctification certainly spoils a man in a proper sense for this world.

We should be thankful, then, that God holds out such warnings and signals along the way of departure, so that one can judge himself where he is. As first joy, then liberty, and then power is felt to be going, we are really listening to alarm bells rung by a faithful heavenly hand to arouse us, make us look backward and then upward for the pardoning, purifying and restoring grace that God for Christ's sake is always willing to give.

CHAPTER V.

THE BLESSING CAN BE RECOVERED,

THERE is no doubt that the beautiful and restful grace of sanctification, which many have lost, can be possessed again.

It may be difficult so to convince the one whose heart is empty and aching from the spiritual bereavement that such may be the case, but it is none the less true. The mind is never more painfully fertile than at such a time to recall and construct arguments and illustrations to prove that the present wretchedness must continue, that the loss is irreparable and there is and can be no hope.

Moreover, it is the will of Satan whose devices are numerous and powerful to keep the soul in gloom with a view to its ultimate despair.

One paralyzing thought he delights to urge upon the holiness backslider is that he has sinned against so much light, that there is and can be no pardon for the offense. That the very greatness of the blessing parted with constitutes the enormity of the sin.

So tempest-tossed and bewildered is the backslider, that he overlooks the fact that Satan does not call attention to the magnitude of grace and the almighty power of the Blood to cleanse. The great enemy is simply anxious for the soul to notice the depths of its fall without pointing it to the heights of salvation, nor gracious uplifting power of the Son of God. Happy is the man who at such a time will recall the verse, "Where sin has abounded, grace much more abounds." The blessed thought should thrill us that Divine Love has stooped lower than man fell. "That earth has no sorrow which heaven can not cure."

A second distressing thought presented to the wanderer at this time is the case of Esau. The Tempter gloats over the case as he reminds the man that the Bible itself says that although Esau sought his forfeited blessing "carefully with tears," he could not find it again. He does not tell the sorrowing one that this does not refer to the salvation of the soul, but to Esau's loss, through the sold birthright, of being in the Messianic line. Who believes that God would reject any one who came with tears and repentance asking forgiveness? A temporal blessing may indeed by one act of folly be finally lost, but departed spiritual grace, thank God, can be recovered.

A third discouraging quotation used by the morbid, disconsolate mind at this time, is taken from Hebrews x. 26: "For if we sin willfully after that we have received the knowledge of the truth, there remaineth no more sacrifice for sins."

According to the way the unhappy heart would

interpret this, no man who has ever sinned wilfully after his conversion can be pardoned. This fact is contradicted by daily observation, and by a gracious experience as well. The ground of fear here seems to be built on the words "sin wilfully," when, so far as the writer can see, all sin is wilful. The definition of sin, with which we are all familiar, is that "Sin is the voluntary transgression of the divine law." If we do not intend, desire or will to do a wrong thing, the moral quality goes out of the deed, and we say in explanation that the act was done ignorantly or under compulsion.

It occurs to the author that the main meaning of this verse is entirely overlooked by the spiritually lapsed man, and by many others as well. It does not say there is no more *forgiveness* of sins when we do wrong, but to the wilful sinner "there remaineth no more *sacrifice* for sin." In other words, there is but one Christ. There is no second Saviour or salvation to us who abuse the grace and provision of the atonement of Jesus. The wilful sinner who turns his back on Christ and goes on his ruinous course will find no more altars or sacrifices along the way. He must take Jesus, or be lost. There remaineth no more sacrifice for sins.

A still more distressing passage is brought up by the adversary in Heb. vi. 4-6: "For it is impossible for those who were once enlightened, and have tasted of the heavenly gift, and were made partakers of the Holy Ghost, and have tasted the good word of God and the powers of the world to come, if they shall fall away, to renew them again unto repentance; seeing they crucify to themselves the Son of God afresh, and put him to an open shame."

To this gloomy quotation we reply that the passage refers not to the loss of sanctification, or even salvation, but to the fearful sin of apostasy. It was a dreadful thing in the time when Paul wrote, when the cause of Christ was small and struggling, for a man thus to act. It so shook the faith of thousands, that the act put him beyond the pale of mercy. The man's apostate life equalled a second crucifying of the Lord Jesus.

That this is not the case of the backslider from justification or even sanctification, is evident to one who studies their lives, and marks their gloom and oftentimes crushing sorrow over departure from Christ. So far from feeling like "putting Christ to an open shame," they are ashamed of themselves. Nothing would be more impossible than for them to crucify the Saviour. We have heard some of them say that even if they should finally be lost they would go down to the pit believing in and loving Christ.

The fact remains that the wanderer can come home. He that said to His disciples that as often as a trespassing brother should turn to them, even seven times in a day and say, "I repent," and "thou shalt forgive him," will certainly be no less pitiful than the men He was instructing in mercy.

The apostle said He had "compassion on the ignorant and on them that are out of the way." There are many such to-day who are "out of the way," who once fairly blazed, and glorified God in it. Christ has compassion on them. He can bring them back, and they are welcome to return.

Tell the backslider, says the Lord, "I am married unto him." Was there ever a tenderer message? Again he says, "I will heal their backsliding. I will love them freely; for mine anger is turned away from him." What more could be said? What more could be desired? What better thing could be done?

So every wanderer can come back. And not only is this true, but backsliders from holiness do get back.

If we had no other case than that of John Fletcher, this alone should inspire the heart of every despondent one with new hope. Read in the Life of Hester Ann Rogers his own testimony in regard to it: "I have received this blessing four or five times, but I grieved the Spirit of God by not making confession, and as often I let it go. I lost it by not observing and obeying the order of God who hath told us, 'With the heart man believeth unto righteousness and with the mouth confession is made unto salvation,' which latter I neglected." This lost blessing he recovered, and so he speaks again : "Now, my brethren, you see my folly. I have confessed in your presence, and now I resolve in your presence also, henceforth I will confess my Master to all the world. And I declare unto you in the presence of God, the Holy Trinity, I am now dead indeed unto sin," etc., etc.

If Fletcher could get it back, then every one can who reads their lines. God has no favorites, and is without partiality or respect of persons. You may have sinned, but Christ is a greater Saviour than you are a sinner. You may have fallen low in hope, faith and life, but Christ can get underneath you and lift you up.

The writer has gone all over in the United States in evangelistic labor. There has scarcely been a place but he found some man or woman who had lost this "pearl of great price," the blessing of entire sanctification. In different ways it had been forfeited. Sometimes it had been lost through failure to testify publicly. Sometimes a fretting or fault-finding spirit had been indulged and Jesus left them. Sometimes they had been betrayed into sin. A number said that they did not know of anything especially wrong that they had done, but the blessing seemed to, "leak out."

With rare exceptions we saw these sad-faced, mute-tongued people recover the departed grace, and the word Ichabod was displaced for Ebenezer.

One we remember stood up at a large camp-meeting in New England and confessed the loss of the blessing. Looking at us with tear-filled eyes she said,

"Empty is the nest
Where the Dove had rest,"

and sat down a picture of woe amid the general sympathy of the large audience. But we all saw the Dove come back to the nest that very week, and the sorrowful face was transfigured with light and joy.

At another time we heard a gentleman in a testimony meeting lament his loss of the blessing. His words impressed all, and particularly one sentence sank deep when he said: "I have not laughed in my heart for three years." What a picture of soul-sadness written in those simple but touching words. Sunlight, laughter, merriment, music all around him, yet his heart in the midst of it all had not laughed in three years! But three days after that I saw him under the glorious light of the recovered blessing, when not only his heart but his lips were overflowing with laughter as well.

In a Southern State we found a gentleman at the altar, bowed down in grief as well as in posture, seeking to find again the pearl of perfect love and rest he had lost. Day after day he was the first to come to the altar and the last to leave. But every line of the face showed hopelessness, and the voice itself had a despairing ring that even affected strong, bouyant altar workers about him. One day the writer looking steadily at him said: "My brother, do you know why you are not able to get the blessing back?"

The man heaved a sigh, gave an upward look of questioning interest, and said: "No, I do not; what is it?"

The preacher laid his hand gently on the shoulder of the seeker and said kindly: "It is because you will not forgive yourself for having lost it." The head of the seeker instantly sank down on the altar before him, while the preacher added: "God is willing to forgive you. He says so in His Word; but you will not forgive yourself."

The preacher left him, for he had covered the case. The man saw the truth, felt it, and that very day "forgave himself," looked to Christ, touched the cleansing blood and swept back into the old-time light and gladness.

Yes; we can get the blessing back. Let the heart-cheering truth be taken up with golden trumpets, silver bugles, beating drums and clashing cymbals. Let some angelic voice in the sky that can be heard all around the world cry out, "Though sin abounds yet grace much more abounds," and the whole race thunder out a hallelujah of thanksgiving as they gather from these words the possibility of return from all sin and spiritual loss and wandering unto God.

Usually, the Saviour will be found where we left Him. If disobedience was the cause of the trouble, the thing to do is to begin to obey again. If the tongue has been silent, go to testifying. If anything has been taken from the altar, put it back, and then stand before the Lord, with tears, prayers, and the humble, patient, expectant waiting of faith until the fire falls. It will fall. God is faithful who has promised, and will not disappoint us.

Let it be remembered that the blessing was obtained at first through consecration, faith and prayer. If lost it can be regained by taking the same steps. Get on the altar; it has not lost its power. Go to believing; faith still unlocks the skies. Pray for the descending fire and witnessing Spirit. They are certain to come if we pray on and "pray through."

We rejoice at the number we have seen get back into this blessing after a time of spiritual loss, and even darkness and falling into sin. How glad they were, how bright they looked, and how happy we all were to see them once more in the Inner Sanctuary called the Holiest, with its beautiful, perpetual light on their faces, its manna in their hearts, and the thick curtains of its spiritual stillness falling all about them.

As an additional word of comfort to those who have been thus restored, we would say that we have noticed that when people recover this blessing, they hold it with increased carefulness and faithfulness. Knowing the value of the grace which had been lost; knowing now better than ever before what it is to have a pure heart, a soul at rest with Christ abiding within, they now guard the treasure with a diligence and prayerfulness surpassing all the watchfulness and devotion of the past.

CHAPTER VI.

HOW TO KEEP THE BLESSING.

IN one sense the blessing of sanctification keeps us. Hence it is very properly called "the keeping blessing." The constant indwelling of Christ, the easy exercise of faith, the restfulness and inner steadfastness of the experience, are all delightful features of the life, and contribute as well to its perpetuity.

The statement that sanctification is more easily kept than regeneration, seems quite incredible to some people. They wonder how a higher life and deeper grace can be more easily retained than a less exalted experience. The explanation is that inbred sin, the disturbing factor and bosom foe of the regenerated man, is cast out in the work of sanctification. The internal war is over. The battle is now on the outside. The life feels as if it was self-perpetuating. There is no fag or let-down in it, because Christ is ever in the heart. Brimful of holy energy it is always aggressive, and in addition has such unfoldings and disclosures of new strength and sudden developments of power which thrill the possessor, and can only be explained by the indwelling presence of the Son of God. At once on awakening in the morning the man feels the blessing stirring in his soul. With every call to duty there is felt a great reserve of strength and a conscious adequacy for the occasion.

Yet, of course, there are things for the sanctified individual to do, and which not to do would rank him with antinomians and fanatics and result disastrously and suicidally to the blessing. There are precautions and observances that must be seen to. We never get beyond the need of means of grace while in this world of probation. Self-denial, cross-bearing, watchfulness and prayer are to be practiced up to the portals of the tomb. To deny and neglect these things is to write ourselves down as moral idiots and bring danger and ruin upon the soul.

The sweet grace of sanctification can be retained. Great and gracious as it is, there is no need of losing it. The author has enjoyed the experience for seven years. He knows of a lady who has possessed it unbrokenly for fifty years, and he heard an aged servant of God say once that he had enjoyed it uninterruptedly for sixty-two years.

But these people did something to preserve the grace. For just as neglecting to do certain things has caused the blessing to depart, so the doing of certain things commanded us will retain the gracious experience. There are several things which, if observed and practiced, will prevent all spiritual lapse and plant the blessing in us like a towering and immovable mountain.

The first is faith. We obtain sanctification by faith, but it is also retained by faith. Faith is the vital point of union with Christ, and, of course, Satan makes his strongest assaults at this point. If after the reception of the blessing he can make the soul doubt its presence or continuance, he at once secures a foothold again in the territory from which he was ejected, and will soon rob the heart of its birthright and treasure.

It is noticeable that immediately after a person has received the witness of the Spirit to sanctification, the Adversary charges down upon the soul with his doubts. It is well for all such assaulted individuals to remember that just as soon as the Son of God received the anointing or baptism of the Holy Ghost on the banks of the Jordan, that he was immediately afterwards driven into the wilderness and there tempted forty days by the Devil. He conquered by faith and in the use of the Word of God. We can do the same.

The writer made this discovery on the second day of his sanctification. He found that under the heavy pressure of dark spirits he kept sweet and still in soul by exercising faith and repeating a number of times through the time of spiritual trial the words, "The blood cleanseth me from all sin," and, "The altar sanctifieth the gift." This quiet exercise of faith kept the experience as steady in the soul as a fixed star is in the heaven. He never forgot the victory nor the lesson learned at that time. He found that a quiet, persistent faith will either keep in check or throw off the gloomy and dark influences of Satan as a mountain wall casts off the waves of the sea. That it was a tonic protecting from the malaria of doubt. He discovered that the simple repeating of certain passages of God's Word as quoted above had a strange strengthening effect upon the heart and vitalized the spirit of faith itself. He saw that there was a wonderful reacting influence on each other, the Word on the faith and the faith on the Word. Faith grew stronger by repeating passages of Scripture, and the Word became sweeter and stronger in its meaning under the increasing faith. In short, he found that Satan is powerless to despoil the soul of the pearl of great price so long as that soul believes God sanctifies it. That when a man drives a stake down here and says, Alabama, "Here we rest," he does rest, and the Adversary has to stand with impotent rage and see the smiling child of God with head anointed, cup running over and eating joyously in the presence of his enemies, whether they be terrestrial or infernal.

Many of those who have lost the blessing make the confession, "I got to doubting." Who wonders at the loss? As Faith is the condition of the reception and retention of grace, then, of course, Doubt, which is its opposite, is the way to lose all we have. All sin and spiritual lapse is preceded by doubt. It opens the door to Satan and he rushes in to sow tares in the wheat, and possess the house again which had been swept and garnished.

But faith keeps the door of the heart; faith retains the grace and presence of God, and makes it impossible for the devil to do his work. And so the just not only shall, but do, live by faith.

A friend of the writer was sanctified one day, and three days afterward the powers of darkness came down upon him and the Satanic whisper was fairly hissed into his soul: "You know you are not sanctified." But this time the great Enemy bore down upon one who was ready and able through grace to meet him. His reply was, "Is that so? Then if I am not sanctified, here goes again. My all is on the altar; the altar sanctifies the gift. I am the gift and, therefore, I am sanctified. Hallelujah!" And lo! as suddenly as he came Satan left him.

From a lady friend he did not so soon depart. For several days after she received the witness of the Spirit to her sanctification the devil violently assailed her. Passing her several times during the time of her faith trial we saw the hunted, distressed and puzzled look in her eyes. She could not understand why this tight spiritual pressure should be on her. She did not remember that after the glorious experience on the banks of Jordan came the wilderness trial to Christ. There was no time to talk with her, so I gave her an encouraging smile and grasp of the hand, saying, "All will be well; hold on by faith." She did hold on, quietly exercising a childlike trust until suddenly the Saviour appeared, scattered her tormentors, and angels came and ministered unto her. She obtained the lesson of her life, and to-day has no trouble in going through these character tests, but moves calmly and brightly through them all like a star through the night.

It is wonderful how quickly the lesson of faith is learned which retains the experience of holiness. At first it may be an effort to exercise the belief and go on repeating the Word of God, especially when the joy of the soul may have run low or departed. But in a few hours or days one becomes established in the grace, there is a spirit or whisper of trust in the heart, and the soul settles down with a delightful sense of recumbency upon the love, power and protecting care of the Son of God.

It is now that the man sees the tremendous force of faith as by it he retains the greatest experience of the Christian life. He can now mentally exercise it. It seems to be the breath of his soul and is exhaled like breath. Instead of words being uttered, the thought itself is uppermost, "The blood cleanses me," "Jesus sanctifies me."

Still, while it may be hard at times to repeat those passages of God's Word which bear upon the soul-cleansing power of the blood, yet there is peculiar blessedness in such oral testimony and confession of the lips. In our own experience we have never had to repeat such words as "The blood cleanses me," "The altar sanctifies me," "Jesus saves me now," more than the third time before feeling the sense of victory in the soul, and hearing an inward hallelujah voiced by the answering Spirit who thus assured us that all was well.

The expression "exercising faith" means much. But it is a simple truth for all the blessedness it brings. Men know what it is to exercise their lungs and arms and body, but seem bewildered when we tell them to exercise faith. If we exercise the voice or limbs we *use* them. So to exercise faith we use it, trot it out, whirl it around, and propel it upward. Every effort makes it easier to do, and from uttering the words, "The blood cleanses," "Jesus sanctifies me," the soul gets so that, as we said before, it actually *thinks* these sentences of life. The heart literally broods on the atoning blood, and a feeling of trust encompasses the life like the mountains stand about Jerusalem.

One night at a preaching service we noticed the

minister, who was a sanctified man, with head bowed and lips moving. It was during a protracted meeting and was one of those times when the air seemed to be full of evil spirits. The congregation appeared frozen, and the very atmosphere depressing. We thought that the preacher was praying, as we observed the motion of his lips and caught indistinct whispers. After the service was over we asked him if this was not the case. His reply was:

"No; I was not praying."

"What, then, were you doing?"

With the greatest seriousness and a tone that deeply impressed us he replied:

"I was exercising faith!"

In a flash, then, I saw what a battle he had been going through; and that there in the pulpit he had met the devil and whipped him out by whispering passages of the Word of God and by the exercise of faith. There was a great victory that night in the sermon and at the altar, and this was the way it was won. What this brother did in the meeting and vanquishing of the difficulties of that night, we are to do with every spiritual trial and doubt flung in our way by men and devils. We are to *believe through them* into light.

Let no man who ever saw a person flash a lantern up a dark alley and make it a path of light from end to end, say he does not know what it is to exercise faith. It is to throw a headlight of belief on God's Word and work through a tunnel of spiritual gloom. It bores its way through the devil's suggestions and lies. It turns an X-ray on a wall of dark circumstance and reveals God on the other side. It steadily refuses to doubt the statement of God's Word and the witness of His Spirit. It says that light or no light, sensation or no sensation, feeling or no feeling, knowledge or no knowledge, when God says a thing is so, it is so. That this settles the matter finally and forever.

We fail to see how Satan can find entrance, much less be able to rob the soul of its greatest treasure when such a faith stands guard with unsleeping vigilance at the door. This is the victory that overcometh low spirits, a sinking heart, whispers of the devil and all the discouragements of this lower world—even our faith.

The second thing necessary to keep the blessing of sanctification is obedience.

Faith is the heart condition, obedience is the life condition. If there is true faith within there will be obedience to God without. They walk together and they go down together. When faith fails disobedience sets in. When obedience fails faith sickens and will die if the course is persisted in.

When consciously disobedient to God faith feels paralyzed for the time, and the lips seem unable to frame the words, "The blood cleanses me now from all sin."

We do not mean to say that the blessing of sanctification is lost by one small act of disobedience, or by two or three such. We certainly believe that by a single act of murder or adultery the blessing would be forfeited. But there are failures of duty that may not be compared to these two sins. Grave as is any act of disobedience be it small or great in its nature, yet we can not believe that God suddenly leaves a man forsaken and cursed for one such omission or commission. We believe that sanctification, like regeneration, as a rule, departs gradually. As the light fades out of the sky, so the glory leaves the soul. First joy goes, then liberty, and then the testimony. The man has become dumb. Satan has again locked the lips, the daughters of music are gone, and the old heart burden has come back. The blessing has leaked out, as some of them say. Yes, and it leaked out through acts of disobedience.

Disobedience is a grave thing. We know a lady now eighty years of age who says that she deliberately disobeyed God fifty years ago, after having been a sanctified woman for several years. She says that while God forgave her and she has not lost the blessing, yet her sanctified experience has never been the same. We believe that she has allowed Satan to keep her crushed down by this memory, when the atonement covers the whole thing and she should have gone free; but the fact that the memory of the act has so burdened her all through life shows the gravity of a single deed of disobedience. If we would keep the blessing of sanctification we must obey God. His Word must be kept. We can not violate His commandments. We must hearken to His calls and follow His leadings. He can unmistakably impress His will upon us, and if we do it not, we will be certain to get into trouble.

We do not mean that every impression that comes to the mind is of God. Some of them are so far from being of heaven that we will please God by not paying any attention to them. He says, "My sheep know my voice," and that voice will sound in His Word, in His Providence, and in the whisper of the Spirit to the heart, guiding, restraining, teaching and leading.

We must obey God. What a joy it brings to the soul to be thus consciously submissive and doing the whole will of God. What a ring to the voice and what an added power to the life it brings. Satan feels helpless before a man with faith in heart and perfect obedience to God in life. In a word, we must "trust and obey," and in doing so will be invincible.

There is a lovely little hymn which bears the name "Trust and Obey." The chorus runs,—

> "Trust and obey
> For there's no other way,
> To be happy in Jesus
> But to trust and obey."

Neither is there any other way to retain the grace of sanctification but by this same Faith and Obedience.

The third essential is seen in "The Blood." The instant there is a conscious spiritual hurt we should fly to the blood of Christ and claim its immediate application. It is better not to lose time in argument or inquiry as to whether the act was wrong or not which brought the disturbed state of mind and heart. Better fly at once to the blood, obtain the instantaneous cleansing, and settle the other matters afterward.

Few realize the ever-present power of the blood of Christ. It "cleanseth," says John. It cleanses instantly, and it cleanses now, the very moment we claim its virtue by faith.

There is no need to be in condemnation a moment in case of sins of ignorance and surprise. The blood is available every second. Even in matters of graver nature, it is through lack of knowledge of the present power of the blood, that makes the man postpone his soul cleansing and recovery until certain mental agonies, fervent supplications and physical humiliations shall have been gone through with.

The Bible does not say that the blood and something else cleanseth, but *The Blood!* So, if the world to-day would renounce its beads, pilgrimages, and works of righteousness, and look to the blood of Christ, it would be saved. If Christians would turn their gaze from the thought of growth, development and church work to the purifying blood of Jesus, the heart purity or holiness they desire would be instantly given. If sanctified people who have lapsed more or less in the sanctified life, and are trying to work their way back into the old-time favor and honor of Heaven would only look to "The Blood," they would find themselves instantly healed, restored, cleansed, filled and fired again.

In recognition of possible weakness, mistakes and missteps; in view of the fact that some fiery dart of the evil one may pierce the Christian armor, God has provided the ever-present, ever-powerful, ever-cleansing blood of Christ. The instant that the soul is wounded it should fly at once, without the loss of a second, to the Saviour, and cry, Lord Jesus, apply thy blood ; and it should stay at His feet until it is done.

This is not Antinomianism, abusing the grace of God, and sinning that mercy might abound ; but a proper faith that comes at once to the Saviour when betrayed into sin. The spirit that would tarry and bemoan the past with profitless groans and paralyzed activities is not that which is enjoined in the Bible. It is not the act that most exalts God and His plan for our redemption.

That which honors Christ and His salvation is the immediate return to the Lord in case of departure, and the instant appropriation of the blood which cleanses through and through, and now, and for evermore.

CHAPTER VII.

SOME FEATURES OF THE SANCTIFIED LIFE.

THERE is such a life. We are ushered into it on compliance with the conditions of consecration and faith, that stand like a great portal, barring out and yet opening in. With the experience of an instantaneous sanctification rushing into the soul, the sanctified life begins.

Of course there is skepticism with some about the individuality and distinctiveness of the life; but this doubting comes from those who have not gone through the portal. One can not know how a garden really looks until he enters the gate and strolls down the walks. He may have had descriptions and so formed ideas, but all know how every description comes short of the reality; and the road, lane, field, city, or landscape that has been portrayed with pen or tongue is always different from the mental conception when we see it.

Men may smile as they will over the statement that the sanctified life or experience differs from that of regeneration, but such smiles can not and do not alter facts. These persons in their derision simply show that they have not "entered in."

Every life different from our own is necessarily a mystery. A worm is a tiny thing, and men may write learnedly about its sensations, but the fact remains that most of what is written is mere conjecture. The only way to know how a worm feels is to become a worm. So a bird can be held in or crushed by the hand. Some persons have written volumes on the habits and feelings of birds. But all written is the opinion of a being on the outside of the little songster. He can not know how a bird feels; to do that he must become a bird.

In like manner we study the angels. Much has been said about them, but how little is really known of their habits, labors, and joys? We have to study them from the outside. They constitute a different order of beings from the human race, and are never to become men and women, just as we are never to become angels. We may affect great wisdom in writing about this heavenly order, but, after all, it is merely speculation. The only way to know how an angel feels is to become an angel.

The unconverted man looks at the regenerated man and thinks he understands him. He hears the Christian say that he "feels good and happy," and his reply is, "So do I." It would be very hard to convince him that the good feeling of the child of God runs on spiritual lines, while his moves on the physical. This very explanation would fail to explain to him or convince him. His idea of "feeling good" is mainly animal. He has, for instance, eaten a hearty meal, and now in dressing robe and slippers, stretched in an easy chair, cigar in mouth, he sits in lazy, dreaming mood, looking into the fire. He says he "feels good"; but any one can say that the entire sensation is purely animal. That it is a puppy-dog enjoyment, a cat-on-the-rug contentment. The child of God tells him that if he repents and believes on the Lord Jesus Christ, he will have a good feeling to sweep through the soul so much purer, better and nobler, that the other would not be worthy to be mentioned in the same breath.

Is it not strange that a regenerated man who can see these things, and can recognize the error of the unconverted in this matter should fall into a similar mistake when he sits in criticism and judgment on the life of the sanctified man? He hears him give his experience, and straightway asserts that he has all that the sanctified man possesses. Of course the person who has had the baptism of the Holy Ghost knows better, but is equally well aware that no human word or power can convince the converted man to the contrary; that this is the work of God. It takes the Holy Ghost, with the Word, to divide soul and spirit, joints and marrow, discern the depths of the heart, expose inbred sin, and reveal in startling light the difference between the two works of grace. So the sanctified simply says in reply to the regenerated man that if he consecrates perfectly, believes unwaveringly, and prays importunately that the fire will fall and he will know for Himself this secret of the Lord, which only the Lord can reveal. In other words, "If any man will do His will He shall know of the doctrine." Thus while it takes the Holy Ghost to convince him as He illumines the mind and reveals the deep things of God; still it is the duty of the sanctified man to stand firm for his experience and emphasize the distinctiveness and superiority of the work of grace. God will use that humble, faithful testimony not only for the good of the testifier, but make it "light sown for the righteous" which, under the divine blessing, will yet spring up in the conviction and purification of the believer.

There is then such a thing as the sanctified experience. There is, thank God, a sanctified life. It must be so recognized by the honest observer, and it is felt with thrills of joy by the possessor himself, who knows better than any one else its marked contrast to the former religious experience, and its blessed superiority at every point.

A volume might be written here, but we content ourselves with calling attention to several features of what we call the sanctified life or experience.

Perhaps the prominent feature is inward rest. The soul has been stilled and remains still. The spirit of worry is gone. There is a sweet disinclination to fret. An atmosphere of calm pervades the breast and penetrates the life. It abides steadily through the day, no matter what that day holds for us in the shape of labor, burdens, unpleasant people, and trying circumstances. There is no delight over the trying circumstances themselves, but a restfulness of soul in spite of them. Paul did not give thanks *for* everything, but said: "*In* everything give thanks." It certainly would be a novel experience to many Christians to begin and end the day calmly; to wake up in the morning with a sweet serenity of spirit, and to go through each new day with a deep, still peace, whose steady flow delights as well as astonishes him. And yet this is the plain promise of God, "Quietness and assurance forever," and this is the experience of a great and ever-increasing number in the land. One of these, a lady friend, said to the author: "I am kept amazed at the inward rest and stillness of my soul. I never dreamed there was such a sweet peace for me, and I am disposed to wonder if there can be any mistake about it all. Ought I not to be more concerned about different things; and where is the ecstatic joy I felt in the first few weeks of the blessing?" She, in other words, under that word "concerned" was marveling over the absence of the old "fret" that used to be in her, and also failed to see that the great peace she now had was simply *joy boiled down.*

A second feature is that of a spirit of praise. Every child of God is conscious of this at times, but there are serious gaps and intervals when it is not felt. Moreover, the hour when it is realized, as a rule, in the regenerated life is one which abounds in helps and external causes of inspiration. All is going on well in the individual heart, family circle and church life. The meeting is being blessed, the work is succeeding, and faith has turned to sight. Well in body, well in soul, and everybody around us well—now, then, let us praise God. We simply ask here who could not do so under such circumstances?

The gift and grace we speak of under this head is a spirit of praise which abides in the soul under all circumstances. The inner bubbling of gladness is felt not simply when all is well, but when things are not well. It gushes up in the face of coldness, opposition, detraction, and wrong. It sings in spite of loneliness, and pain of heart and body. It praises God in the face of apparent failure. It can be cast off by loved ones and separated from the company of friends, and yet keep rejoicing. It can walk around the walls of Jericho thirteen times without seeing a crack, and yet shout. It can be unjustly condemned, whipped, put in a dungeon, and behold! at midnight it will burst into hosannas. It can, and does, cry hallelujah at all times.

The first two sanctified preachers the writer met

impressed him with this spirit of rejoicing. He heard them say repeatedly in the Conference room and elsewhere: "Glory to God!" "Praise the Lord!" "Hallelujah!" This spirit, life and language was beyond the author of this book at that time, and his judgment of the phenomenon was that these utterances had first been genuine, but by frequent repetition had become mechanical, and that nothing but the expression of a mental habit was now before him; or, in other words, here were parrot-like utterances in the religious life. Two years after the writer obtained the same blessing possessed by these men of God, and found to his delight and astonishment that it was not a parrot at all, but a nightingale singing its very heart out on a rose bush in a moonlight night. He found there was a blessing which, when received in the soul, bubbles up in a tender holy joy, wreathes the lips with smiles, puts a shine on the face, a sparkle in the eye, and issues from the tongue in words and expressions of praise.

The wife of a minister received the blessing of sanctification in a gracious meeting held by the writer. She had been soundly converted, and was a faithful worker in the church. But she felt that disposition within to fret and worry over household and other matters. The sound of a dog barking at night was especially objectionable and trying to her. She called it nervousness. The night following the day she received the blessing she could not sleep for the happiness which filled her. She said that the watch dog seemed possessed that night and barked for hours, but with her joy-attuned nature she heard the sound with new ears; the discordant sound was gone, and the dog seemed to say, "Praise God!" "Praise God!" Next morning while in the kitchen arranging things for breakfast she, by an unwitting movement of the hand, brought down a whole pile of tin and iron vessels with a great clash and clatter. Two days before it would have been intolerable and upsetting; but with the holy joy and praise now welling up richly in her soul, she clapped her hands and cried out with shining face, "O the music! O the music!"

A third feature in the life of the sanctified is the blessed consciousness of a perfect love. Perfect not in the sense that it may not grow stronger and more intense as the years go by, but perfect as regards the absence of things contrary to love imbedded in the heart. It is a pure love. The former temporary hates, jealousies, envyings and bitterness toward certain people are all gone. A gentle, tender, loving feeling is in the heart for all men. This does not mean that we love all alike. This would be unnatural and impossible. There is a general love for the whole Race, peculiar affections for those naturally near to us, and special likings and attachments to others, who, by nature, temperament and character, draw us toward them. Yet to all different classes there is felt a pure, genuine love, although the love may vary in character and intensity.

On the Godward side we are thrilled to discover that the love we now bear Him is not now mixed as it had formerly been, and is supreme at all times. It is sweet and blessed beyond words to describe, to feel the perfect love for God nestling in and warming the heart continually. King David is on his throne, the Absalom of rival affections is dead, and the kingdom within lies all fair, peaceful and beautiful, without a note of discord and a sign of insurrection.

Such a condition of soul, is found in its tenderness to all people, to prevent the fault-finding and uncharitable speech; while the same tongue in speaking of God and things divine almost insensibly, and yet naturally, is drawn into simple, unaffected and reverential language. Cheerfulness takes the place of levity, kindness displaces harshness, and from the lips that once found fault with God and assailed man, come the breathings of the loyal soul that find utterance in praises and ejaculations of love to God, and fervent "God bless yous" to the children of men. And it abides. The fitfulness or fluctuation seen in the regenerated life is no more. The blessed experience is that of being fixed, grounded, rooted, settled in love.

A fourth feature is the working spirit, or desire

and effort to do good. The instant the disciples received this grace they flew to the fields and vineyards of God. Two thousand years after I saw the same blessing fall upon a lady at the altar. I heard her cry, "O my husband!" saw her spring to her feet, rush into the audience, seize hold of the now tremendously convicted man, lead him to the altar, and in an agony of prayer and triumph of faith lay hold now on God, and behold! salvation came down. The two works between that of the disciples and this woman was different in regard to magnitude of operations, but the same spirit was at work. Not all are called to public work, but those who have this blessing find work to do, and gladly do it. They feel strangely and powerfully wound up to do it. It may be laid out by the divine hand in a very obscure corner or restricted sphere; it may be a simple *enduring* at times, and which will be a doing of the highest order; it may be a marching to-day and a standing still to-morrow. God knows, and He will direct, and the sanctified soul will obey. The spirit of the working Christ abiding in us is bound to lead out in words and deeds that will bless the world in some way, and help to restore the departed Paradise.

Figures of a wound up and going machine, steam pulsating in cylinders, and the prophetic description of fire burning in the bones come to the mind in describing this divinely inspired activity. The curve of the bow, the tautness of the string, the poise of the arrow, the coil of the spring are all felt when truly filled and empowered of God in sanctification. Such an one can not be idle. In some way, in small things or in great things, and in his or her own line and way, the sanctified person must and will work for God.

A striking feature about it is that this work does not seem to exhaust. The soul remains fresh. There is a bouyancy felt throughout which delights the worker and gives moral force to the performance in the eyes of beholders. The soul is never so full of rest as when engaged in this unfailing activity for heaven.

We remember a Bible picture of the seraphim, where they are represented with wings in swift movement, while their bodies were motionless. It is a striking illustration of the two-fold experience of work and rest in the sanctified life. High pressure work of brain and body, and profound calm and rest of soul. The man works now for God as he never did before, but he also rests at the same time with a depth and sweetness equally remarkable.

A fifth feature of the life is the delightful consciousness of being kept. It is difficult, if not impossible, to bend any set of words around the circle of this experience, or find sentences that can penetrate the intricacies of the grace as it affects the heart and life. Like a road has to be traveled to be known, so must the soul journey on this delightful way to know of what we are speaking. Possession of the blessing is the only key to the understanding of this gracious mystery.

The author had read the word in the Bible, "Kept by the power of God," and had heard it used by some who had a strange, sweet light on their faces, and a glad, exultant ring in their voices, but he failed to comprehend what they were talking about until at last he finally became an "overcomer" and obtained the "white stone, and in the stone a new name written, which no man knoweth saving he that receiveth it."

A kept life! Figures of restfulness, repose and protection arise at once to the mind; a child in the arms of its mother, a sealed fountain, a walled city, and yet all fail to measure up descriptively to this strange, sweet experience of the sanctified soul, that we call being "kept." It is a spiritual sensation as distinct as the feeling of pardon. It sustains all through the trying hours of the day, is the last thing felt in the heart as we fall asleep, and the first realized in the soul on awakening in the morning. If this was the only feature of sanctification, it would pay ten thousand times over to obtain the blessing.

This chapter is a condensed statement of some of the features of the sanctified life. No one can read them without seeing it is a distinct experience; and any one hearing of such a life should never be content until he came into the same blessedness.

CHAPTER VIII.

THE LONELINESS OF THE LIFE.

THERE are many paradoxes in the spiritual life. In the expression, "Alone, yet not alone," we find one of them.

The Saviour was in one sense the most solitary of men, and yet in another he was not lonely. He said to His disciples at one time, "Will ye also go away?" and then added that he was not alone, for the Father was with Him. He who was in unbroken intercourse with the Father, and had angels ascending and descending upon him, never knew such a thing as men do of the heaviness of his own company or the oppressiveness of solitude. He was adjusted by His perfect life and nature to every condition and surrounding, and was full of rest everywhere.

The sanctified life being God-centered, and having Christ abiding within, satisfying every longing of the heart, can not be lonely in the sense that men use the term. Ennui is impossible with a soul full of the Holy Ghost. Every minute has its charm, every occurrence brings or is made to bring a blessing, the day has its glory, the night its songs, solitude its sweetness, and God is seen and felt in everything.

The old-time necessity, forcing one to take hat or bonnet and run off in social gossip to get rid of an hour or two that hangs heavily on their hands, becomes an unknown experience. The social life is not despised nor given up, for Duty still calls in this direction, but the visit is now undertaken in a new spirit, and one's room or home is not left because its stillness and quiet can not be borne.

The sanctified life is not lonely in the true and high sense of the word. It brings a spiritual and heavenly companionship that made Patmos an antechamber of heaven to John, turned a bastile dungeon into a place of beauty and glory to Madam Guyon, and transforms the room of the invalid into a sanctuary of rest, fanned with angel wings and lighted up with the smile of Christ.

But in another sense the sanctified life is lonely. As viewed by the world it is painfully lonely, but as felt by the sanctified person himself it is lonely without painfulness.

There is a growing recognition of the fact of this separation and solitariness and a consequent shrinking from the experience upon the part of some, and an endeavor to so shift, change and adjust the life as to deliver the individual from that same dreaded feature of loneliness. This, of course, is done mainly by those who have not received the grace of sanctification, and so can not understand it. But there are

LONELINESS OF THE LIFE.   91

also those who have entered "into the holiest" and have not studied the truth itself and its relations and demands as they should. So they are found in their efforts trying to win, conciliate, and keep up old relations, to improve Bible nomenclature and to fill up chasms dug between men in the spiritual life by the Holy Ghost. The result of this has been disastrous to the experience they professed. They regained their old company and associations, but they lost the blessing. They wanted to bring it from its marble pillar of flagellation, from its solitary position of suspicion and rejection, from its star-like shining far above the flaring candles of earth, but in doing this the blessed Form disappeared, the star vanished, and the glory went out.

We might as well come to the knowledge of the Truth, act accordingly, and be saved any more failures of a heart-breaking nature. If we want this swan of the skies to sing and float high in our hearts, we must not try to make it like the other fowls in the barn-yard. We must take it as it is. It is a blessing beyond all price in value, it is a life the sweetest of all under the sun, but coupled with this is the feature of a peculiar loneliness. We had better not divide asunder that which God hath joined together.

Let it be understood once for all that the loneliness we speak of is not a Pharisee separatism which holds itself better, and will have nothing to do with other classes of religious people. Nor is it the exclusiveness of a hide-bound bigotry, nor a timid shrinking from all social life, nor the repetition of the ghastly mistake of the Dark Ages when the church judged that the highest piety could not be developed in the daily walks of life and hence removed to the shadows and silence of the monastery and convent.

No such unnatural, unhealthy and un-Christian loneliness is taught by the Bible and wanted by the world. The genuinely sanctified man is a social man in the best sense of the word. He is in touch and sympathy with all classes of people, and, like his Lord, is found in the market-places as well as the synagogue, and, like Him, always doing good.

The loneliness we speak of is to be found in other directions.

First, sanctification has to be sought in a solitary way, or isolation from the world for the time being.

The disciples separated themselves from every pursuit and from the noise and rush of roads and streets and came together in the quiet of the Upper Room. Even then it was ten days before the holy fire descended. What if they had not thus specially removed themselves and given the undivided attention and desire of mind and heart to God. Then it is certain we would never have heard of Pentecost, at least through them.

Jacob in the obtainment of the Peniel Blessing

went out by himself on the brookside. Afar off he could see the twinkling camp-fires, where wives, children and servants rested unconscious of the suffering and sorrowing man who wept and struggled alone all through the long hours of that starlit Syrian night.

It is not only well to be isolated at such a time, but necessary to obtain the revelation of the deep things of God. His voice is "a still small voice," and is not heard in its clearness amidst the world's loud talking, laughter and rush after money and pleasure. Certain instincts of the soul lead us away from the street into the sanctuary, or closet of prayer. And even when in a company of believers, like the case of the disciples, there must be a sinking away from each other and from every surrounding, a separation unto Christ alone, in the fulfillment of the prophet's words, when he says, "Each one mourned to himself apart."

We are confident that the difficulty with many in obtaining the blessing of sanctification is right here. They are not willing to be alone long enough for God to search them, and show them "the ground of their heart," the dark principle within, which when Isaiah saw in the stillness of the Temple while waiting on the Lord, made him cry out, "I am undone."

It pays to wait in solitariness before God. And garrets, cellars, barns, and the silent grove looking down upon kneeling and prostrate figures have witnessed revelations of divine glory that myriads of our cathedral churches know nothing of.

Again, the very announcement of the fact that you are seeking sanctification will produce a remarkable falling away of friends and acquaintances. The loneliness is now not only that of your seeking God in privacy, but a solitarism made by people holding themselves aloof from you in mingled doubt, pity and wonder as to the final outcome of your present proceedings.

But for Gospel explanation this social withdrawal would be as mysterious as crushing. He that seeks sanctification asks only for Christ. He sees that "Jesus only" is necessary for happiness, and seeks alone for Him. He has found that business, pleasure, marriage, money, children, position, honor, travel, having all been tried, fail to satisfy the soul. The aching void is left in the heart. He now wants Jesus only.

This simplification of life, this one desire left out of thousands, lifts the man away from the every-day thought and practice of men. It constitutes a philosophy that is at present beyond them. Being past their comprehension they fall into the mistake that the anxious faced seeker before them is in an abnormal, unhealthy state of mind, in a word, deluded, and can only bring ridicule and failure on himself, and drag them with him into the maelstrom of public remark and judgment, if they are seen to be identified, associated with or in anyway connected with him. Hence in a figurative way the hands are washed, the skirts are shaken, and the feet walk off with those worldly, sensible heads. And from a safe and respectable distance, rows of cool-looking eyes are turned critically, deprecatingly and pityingly upon the religious phenomenon before them at the altar, who wants Jesus and Jesus only. They hear him say he is willing to give up things that they know to be perfectly proper and legitimate; that he surrenders so excellent a thing as reputation, which required them twenty to forty years to build up; that he is willing to be misunderstood, abused, slandered and rejected by friends, family and church itself, if necessary; in a word, they hear uttered many things which, in their earthly wisdom and cool, level-headed judgment and good horse sense they pronounce extravagant, if not fanatical, and so with many misgivings and shakings of the head they leave the man to himself.

Still again, the reception of the blessing of sanctification will cause a final falling away from you not only of acquaintances, friends, church laborers and fellow Christians, but one's kindred and oftentimes family itself.

The man, even with his new-found purity and joy, is at first aghast over this social landslide and the sudden sense of distance and separation from those whom he never loved so tenderly and so well before.

He tries to explain the new life to his friends, and they look at him as if he was talking Sanscrit. He pours out his experience to his family; they listen with outward respect in some instances, with ill concealed amusement in others, with evident sorrow and mortification in still others, and with unbelief in all.

He next goes to old church workers or to the ministry, and with flaming tongue gives his experience and tries to get them to see it. But through all the conversation he is held at arm's length, the faces turned upon him are cold, skeptical, unsympathetic, and there is an evident reluctance to being seen with him on the street, and an equally manifest desire to get away.

After this the man rushes into the religious press if he is allowed, and pours forth the fact of the new found blessing in glowing sentences. Surely all will see it now. But the following issue of the paper contains three articles in reply, one exceedingly bitter, a second ridiculing, and the third in a patronizing and pitying manner, telling the sanctified brother that he, the writer, had received an hundred blessings like the one he had written about, and there was still a thousand left; to keep on and get all he could; that there was no end to God's blessings, and so they could not, and should not be numbered.

Religious correspondence on the same line also

proved a failure. Some letters were answered in a curt spirit, some with an offended, and others with a bored tone. Some remained long unanswered, and still others were never granted a reply.

It was exceedingly hard to give up the friends of a religious life-time, even after all these disappointments and rebuffs; and so effort after effort was still put forth to get in touch with certain church members and ministers with whom in former days he had enjoyed sweet fellowship and prayed, preached, shouted, labored, and won victories for Christ together. But it was all in vain. A chasm had been dug by the Holy Ghost in a distinct work of grace. The love and inclination to be "in touch" was on the sanctified side, the shrinking and distrust was on the other side, and the moral impossibility of coming together was on both sides.

Two letters received in two months of one another from the same individual, but one written before, and the other after the party addressed had received the blessing of sanctification, would fully serve to show the chasm or distance we speak of. Indeed, there is no need to reproduce the letters entire, but simply the opening and concluding lines:

[Before.]

MY WELL BELOVED BROTHER:

I was delighted to receive your letter of the, etc., etc.

, ...

Cordially and affectionately yours,

※ ※ ※

Rev. ———. [After.]

DEAR SIR AND BROTHER :
Yours of the 15th inst to hand, etc., etc.

.   .   .   .

Yours truly,

* * *

This last sent a pang through the heart on its reception, and caused additional wonder to the sanctified man as he realized that he never had entertained a warmer love for all men than now in this time of frosty notes, freezing bows and distant polar region manners.

But wonder or not, the fact remains that the man who obtains the grace of sanctification finds himself held off at arm's length by the church. He is viewed with suspicion, distrust, and even fear. He is regarded as making claims to superior blessings and graces, and thus lauding himself over his brethren. He is supposed to ignore the Bible teaching of growth in grace, and all the melting, refining processes that come with time in the Christian life. He is felt to be presumptuous and arrogant in claiming to have reached at a single bound of faith what his brethren have been toiling after unavailingly along the Growth Route for twenty, thirty and forty years. In a word, in making the claims he does he "reflects on the brethren," or as it is written in the Gospel, "Master, in saying this you speak against us." This, of course, means a permanent landslide of church friends and church people. They will, without doubt, "separate you from their company," and in so doing will feel they have discharged their duty and done God and the church a service. We must remember that they really and honestly regard people claiming sanctification as being deluded and fanatical.

In one of our large Western cities a young married lady obtained the blessing of sanctification in a meeting held by the writer. She had been a great church worker before, and with a number of prominent church women was a member of a tea drinking circle, which bore quite a high sounding name. This circle had weekly meetings, and was migratory in character, so that it was the custom for an executive committee to issue notices to the members of the day, hour, and private dwelling for the next Bon Ton Tea-Drinking Caucus. But on the news flashing around that she had swept into the experience of sanctification, the lady's name of whom we speak was promptly dropped. No notice came to her. She spoke to us about it with eyes moist and a pained tone: "My old friends have all met together this afternoon without me"; then with a flash of joy in her face she added: "But oh, I am so happy, my heart is singing all the time!"

I saw at a glance that she was drinking something better than tea, and was in a higher and more select circle than the Bon Ton Tea-Drinking Sisterhood.

There are far graver separations than this, but the instance serves to illustrate the point in hand and reveal the spirit at work of which we speak.

Finally the loneliness of the sanctified life comes as a result of the work of grace itself.

God Himself by a second work in the soul lifts the individual into another and higher plane of Christian experience and living. There is a deeper knowledge of the heart, and a more intimate union with Christ. There are profounder joys, deeper peace, clearer light, abiding purity and unbroken communion with God. Such a work that gives new views of God, brings the soul out on the victory side of salvation, flings aside the weeping willow and waves a palm branch, quits complaining and whining, and instead rejoices evermore, prays without ceasing and in everything gives thanks; such a divine work that produces as a result so great a change, is bound to lift the man away from the ordinary rank and file of Christians and land him in lonely spiritual altitudes. For the one party to be astonished at this, and the other to fret about it, argues the lack of thought and failure to see certain well known principles at work on earth, as well as a strange forgetfulness of Bible statements.

The loneliness is nothing but character distance. It is a life removed by divine power. A chasm has been dug by the Holy Ghost. Men look across at each other, see each other, but can not touch as of yore, when all were on the same bank or shore of a common experience.

To attempt to bridge or fill up this moral space or gap between yourself and others when it was made by the Spirit of God, is to imperil and lose the grace you enjoy. It is not intended of Heaven that the space should be bridged. The Holy Ghost alone can bring your friends to you. You can not afford to go back where you once were.

Right here is a peril, and here many have lost the great blessing. They felt the loneliness and imagined they could go back and down into the neighborhood of a past grace, that they could discard their Canaan language, hide the new truths they had learned, say nothing of the precious secret, and so ingratiate themselves with their chafed and sore-spirited brethren as to win them. So the logs were hewn, the timbers laid, the passage way constructed and they went back in a sense, and *became as one of them*. But the distressing result was that while they came over to Moab by their bridge, they could not return to Canaan by it. It seemed to work only one way.

Shortly after the writer received the blessing of sanctification, he saw his ministerial brethren looking shy and standing off from him. They actually appeared uncomfortable in his presence. So he with the intention, not of giving up his blessing, but in the hope of showing them that he possessed the same love and friendship for them, was the same man, and they had nothing to fear, thought he would construct a little footbridge and go down to them as of yore. In a word, he had been accustomed to indulge with them in anecdotal conversation of amusing character, in preachers' meeting jocularity, etc. Once it seemed all right. Now he attempted it again as a sanctified man, hoping to win "the brethren." But he got such a look from Christ, and the footbridge shook so dreadfully, that he ran back in a hurry. In other words, he saw that he could not safely bridge the chasm; that to discard the Canaan spirit and language would result in leaving Canaan itself; that he would imperil the blessing he enjoyed by anything like compromise; and that he must accept the loneliness that had come now as a feature of the blessing, as a result of the work of God in his soul.

We have known numbers to remain weak in the sanctified life because of their ignoring the fact we have been enlarging upon; and we have known numbers more who have lost the blessing altogether. They could not understand the loneliness of the life as being the very handiwork of Heaven, and in attempting to get in touch with people spiritually below them, get out of touch with God above them.

We once had a Senator from Mississippi after the

Civil War who was far ahead in his political and social economic views of the commonwealth he represented. Many of his constituency thought from his speeches in Congress that he was untrue to his State and her best interests. There were threats of recalling him. But he kept calmly on. He knew he was right. He was farther up the mountain than his fellow citizens, and his view of the future was clearer and more far reaching. He could not afford to come down. And he did not come down, but held on his way. He knew that in a few years his party adherents climbing up would see as he saw, and then endorse him. He would wait until then. And it all proved as he thought. In ten years the people reached the standpoint he had been on so long before, and saw as he saw, and recognized that they had wronged him. The beautiful thing about it was that he did not come down because they could not, or did not see as he did. He stayed up on the mountain side and waited for them to ascend. They ascended.

We are to do likewise, as sanctified people. We know the doctrine of the second work to be true. We have the experience. It lifts us up into lonely heights. The religious social world is farther down. We call to them in gladness, and tell them what we have found and see. We speak of the widespread landscape, the nearness of heaven, and the cloudlessness of the place we hold. They may misunderstand us ; moral distance accounting for that. They may misjudge us and say we are unsocial, unfriendly and altogether faulty. But we know in whom we have believed, and what we have received. We can not afford to go down because of adverse criticism and unjust judgment. Let them come up where we stand and see for themselves. Many will do this if we are true to God and remain on the heights.

Remember that this very loneliness of life will bring a blessing to men. It is not the man who spends his time in the crowd and merely reflects the opinion, spirit and attainments of men who most benefits the world, but the man who listens to and speaks of things that have their birth beyond and far above the street. John on the lonely Patmos saw more of heaven than the Sanhedrim in Jerusalem.

Such laymen bring the odor of the flowers of Paradise with them into their offices and stores. Such preachers do not waste time in their pulpits on the questions of the day, about which most of their hearers are better posted than themselves, but gladden, revive and bless the audience with answers from heaven, and fresh tidings from the unseen but eternal world. Such writers give us books that are like Gates of Pearl, opening upon the City of God, while the chapters are like heavenly avenues fringed with trees of life and filled with flitting forms of spiritual truth and beauty.

We thank God every day for the conversation,

preaching, writings and lives of these lonely men and women who find "sermons in stones, books in running brooks," thoughts in stars, messages in flowers, see common shrubs by the road aflame and asparkle with divine glory, hear the surf as it thunders anthems of praise on the strand, and behold in the gold and crimson sunset one of the twelve gates of the Eternal City.

Most men note the storm, fire and earthquake that rend the mountain and shake the valleys. But these are they who stand at the entering in of the cave with mantle-wrapped head and hear the still, small voice that escapes the multitude. When they take away the vail to speak we notice that the face is shining. They have heard things that are only spoken in spiritual heights. And when they turn to speak or write or live before us, it is as if we had heard an angel singing in the evening sky, and life becomes invested with deeper and broader meanings, and a divine design is seen everywhere. Sorrow becomes a garment of moral beauty, Sickness and Disappointment methods of weaning the soul from clay, and the Earth itself is seen to be a college for the mind, a training school for spiritual activities, a theater for the display of God's power in grace, and the very ante-chamber or porch of the world of Glory just hidden from us now by a curtain of blue spangled with silver stars.

CHAPTER IX.

PRAYER AND READING.

A DISTINGUISHING trait of the sanctified life is the spirit of prayer. In the regenerated life it come and goes, but in sanctification it abides. We do not mean to say that the individual is always praying aloud, although frequent ejaculatory supplications will escape the lips. Nor do we mean that he is always mentally praying, although even there he far outstrips his converted brother; but we refer to an almost indescribable mood or frame of prayer that lingers and dwells in the heart. Just as a song sung upon a mountain-locked lake echoes and re-echoes, rocks on the billows, is blown about by the breezes, flung back from the hillsides, clings to the willow branches and absolutely seems to refuse to go from the spot; so the spirit of prayer abides in the soul. It remains in spite of everything. It is felt as we read the Word of God, as we look on sin, or sit in meditation before God. It arises in the hour of public worship, and in the rush of the street. It glows on Sunday, but it also burns on Monday. He who has the genuine work of sanctification finds this sweet gift of heaven, this very breath of God in him and upon him. It may be

PRAYER AND READING.   107

more or less ardent according to obedience and devotion, but it is there with all who are sanctified. The dead, flat, prayerless condition of the soul seen at times in the regenerated life, can not be in the wholly sanctified.

Now for the first time we understand the injunction of the apostle to "pray without ceasing." A command that once seemed fairly to mock us. How faithfully we tried it, and misunderstanding the Word, and ignorant of the divine work in the soul that makes the duty not only possible but easy, we finally regarded the commandment as a standard lifted up to inspire one but never to be attained. We failed to see that the unceasing spirit of prayer comes with the second work of grace.

It is not, however, the spirit of prayer we are calling attention to, but the duty of prayer. The one is the gift of God, the other the observance of the man.

It looks strange that there should be need to impress such a duty upon sanctified people who feel in them this prayerfulness or soul of prayer. But there is necessity for just such a stirring up of pure minds by way of remembrance.

There is undoubtedly a presuming by some sanctified people on the blessing of sanctification. It brings to the heart such a spirit of prayer that they take advantage of it and do not observe the prolonged seasons of supplication of which the Bible and holy biographies have so much to say, and that tell with such wonderful result on personal character and the moral history of the world.

There are as many grades of sanctified people as there are spiritual distinctions in the regenerated life. Some sanctified people live much closer to God than others who possess the same blessing; and the explanation is found in the observance or neglect of protracted waiting upon God in the closet of prayer.

The Lord announces himself a jealous God, and He will never give to the soul a blessing that will make it in a sense independent, and able to get along without frequent and deep communings with Himself. He wants the soul to be often in His presence, and when there to linger. The reasons for this are obvious at a glance.

He desires none of His children to possess stale experiences. He commanded fresh oil to be placed in the lamps, and new loaves on the table of the sanctuary. It is the ever fresh manifestation of God to the soul that is so attractive and impressive to the world.

Again, the deep things of the spiritual life are not given to the hurried visitor at the throne of grace, but to the lingerer at the Footstool of Prayer. It is marvelous what secrets such people obtain from the skies. They are ever astonishing others with their beautiful and blessed discoveries in the Bible and kingdom of Grace. They spend so much time on their knees listening at the gates of heaven to what is going on within, that there is no wonder they surprise those religious people who spend most of their time in listening to what people of this world are saying.

Still again a divine Ambassador and Messenger should be in constant touch with his King and Government in order to do them justice and to benefit as well the people to whom he is sent. This is recognized as necessary in the affairs of the kingdoms of this world. A minister of Foreign Affairs, an Ambassador or Envoy Extraordinary would be felt to be making the name and the office a travesty, if he did not keep in closest touch and latest communication with the powers that sent him.

In like manner that servant of Heaven is most effective who has the longest and latest interviews with the Lord and Master who has sent him forth. It is wonderful how little moved and blessed we are under the words of spiritually dried Christians who have not seen Christ in days and weeks, and are running on a bare memory of former times of grace. And equally marvelous how the simplest utterances of men and women given to much prayer invariably move the heart.

Nothing can take the place of protracted prayer as a peculiar means of grace. Sanctification, with its great gift of the spirit of prayer, was never intended of God to release us at this point, but to multiply the seasons and length of our supplications.

By it comes increased knowledge of God, deeper insight in the Word, a profounder acquaintance with the heart, a greater hatred to sin, a mightier love for holiness and souls, a growing boldness in prayer, a more regal faith, and that heavenly authority and power in eye, voice and life that is instantly seen and recognized by the multitude, whether they be religious or irreligious.

We have only to go to the Gospel to find the divine example of the very kind of prayer we are pleading for. Holy as the Saviour was we find Him spending a whole night at a time in supplication. This being the expression of the pure heart and life of Christ, we might well afford to distrust a holiness experience that is content to move along without special and prolonged waitings upon God. It is running the engine on what is called a dry boiler, and it is bound at last to injure the boiler.

Years ago we read that we were so constituted that just in proportion as the knees get soft the heart grows hard, and as the knees grow hard the heart gets soft. We have found it to be so in our own experience and in that of many others with whom we have conversed. In a word, we never enter upon a religious life in this world that releases us from the obligation and necessity of much prayer. Some fancy this to be the case, but a fancy is one thing and a fact is another. Following these will-of-the-wisp fancies they will yet break their hearts over a granite fact of a backslidden life; and as all backsliding begins in the closet of prayer, the meaning of this figure is at once understood by the reader.

One of the early Bishops of our church was full of holy fire and power. He was a prince and prevailer with God and man. When he preached the fire of heaven would fall. Many used to wonder at his spiritual influence. When he was old and feeble, a preacher was assisting him to disrobe for bed. On passing his hand over the Bishop's knees he was struck with the rough, hard feeling of the skin. It was like a great corn on each knee. He asked the Bishop what produced it, when after some hesitation the aged servant of God replied: "It has been done through prayer."

What a revelation of weak religious lives, and what an explanation of powerless pulpits could be made to-day by the examination of the knees of God's people. How soft most of them would be found to be! And how hard at the same time would be some of their words, how stony their feelings and how iron-like and pitiless their decisions and judgments.

Brainard was much given to prayer, spending thus four and five hours a day. Payson also knew how to tarry hours at a time in supplication. Knox was mighty in prayer. Luther prayed three hours daily, and Wesley did the same. All of us know how the world stands indebted to-day to those men for great spiritual blessings and moral uplifts that never would have come, first to them and then afterward to us, but for the fact that they know how to open the windows toward Jerusalem, and kneeling down, steadily look in that direction and wait until something happened. Something always does happen to such waiting. Isaiah says, "They mount up," and when they mount, they make others rise up with them.

Such an importunate man of prayer was Fletcher. Many will remember how once before going to his knees he told his servant to call him at the end of an half hour, as he had an important engagement. Promptly at the time appointed the servant opened Mr. Fletcher's study door and found the man of God with eyes uplifted, countenance rapt, and soul absorbed in earnest communion with Heaven. The servant, unwilling to break upon his devotions, stole softly away and came back an half hour later. But Mr. Fletcher was still in the same absorbed and rapt attitude. Again the servant retired unable to get his consent to disturb the man of prayer, and again returned at the end of the third half hour to find the man of God in the same position and perfectly oblivious of his surroundings and the flight of time. But the servant dared not disobey any longer, but crossing the room to the kneeling preacher, he said:

"Mr. Fletcher, I dislike to disturb you, but you told me to call you at the end of an half hour."

"What," cried Mr. Fletcher, "is it gone already!"

Is it any wonder that this man shook the church of which he was pastor to the center, and that when he preached, God answered by fire from heaven.

It was in full knowledge of the tremendous outgoing force from this practice that the disciples directed the brethren, to look out for certain men to serve tables, "But we will give ourselves continually to prayer."

If we as sanctified people are to retain fresh and bright experiences, if we would march forward to greater victories, if we would even hold our own we must abound in prayer.

A second great duty of the sanctified man is found in religious reading. Here again the breadth, depth and height of the holiness life in the individual is seen to be affected by the practice or neglect of this privilege and duty as well.

Our knowledge of sanctification is that with its entrance as an experience into the soul, there is immediately realized a keen relish for the Word of God and healthy appetite for all spiritual reading. Hence to see people who claim this blessing careless of the study of the Bible, and failing to inform the brain and feed the soul from the wealth of holiness literature now in the providence of God all around us, is to make us marvel, grieve and even doubt concerning such a type of sanctification.

The double desire to be informed of the truth and delivered from ignorance and error, should be sufficient to cause sanctified people to read the Scriptures and all available good books with avidity. In addition to this the very importance and momentousness of the doctrine calls for proper study and faithful investigation.

Sanctification claims to be the central idea of Christianity, the crowning doctrine of revelation, the moving force of the church, the qualification for service, and fitness for heaven. With such bearings upon the individual, the church and the world itself, ought we not to seek to inform ourselves thoroughly in regard to this great privilege of the soul by going deep into the Word, and culling that literature which has proceeded from the pens of others who have penetrated deeper into the Bible than we have gone ourselves?

If the doctrine is false, let us find it out. If it is true, we owe it to God and our souls to learn all we can about it. In either case, we should read.

We have observed that when fanaticism has made its appearance in connection with the Holiness Movement, it has been where there was false teaching and pernicious literature. Ignorance has ever been and will ever be a hot-bed for error. Lift up the truth and folly and extravagance have to go. Holy Fire is able to destroy fox fire, wild fire and false fire.

We have noticed that in those communities where, after a gracious holiness revival, a great many good books were bought, excellent religious papers subscribed for, and the Bible brought forward at once in faithful, daily study, that such towns and places were singularly free from "isms" of every kind. The magicians failed to put in their appearance with their rods, and if they did, the rod of Truth would promptly swallow up the rods of error.

Most thankful has the writer ever been, that immediately following upon his sanctification, he purchased every first class book on the doctrine and experience he could find. The blessed result in his mind and heart and on his life could not be estimated. At once he was made wise to recognize and avoid error in its various forms; while the various phases and aspects of the experience, the privileges and duties of the life became so quickly familiar as to give him every advantage and start him off with songs, assurances and victories that could and never would have been his but for this same diligence in the matter of reading.

In addition to the thought of instruction is the fact of spiritual food. Devotional reading is a necessity. The soul must have it. Solid spiritual literature meets this want. To deprive the heart of that, is like denying bread and meat to the body. That spiritual starvation makes a weak Christian ought no more to surprise a person than that lack of material food makes a feeble body.

Every Christian with any experience at all knows the effect of newspaper reading and the world's literature upon the soul. What a dry, empty, unfed, unrefreshed, unrenewed and unsatisfied feeling is left in the heart after hours of such reading; while in spiritual books and papers, the soul at once recognizes its nutriment and ends each mental meal with a feeling of strength and satisfaction that is seen in the eye, is read in the face and is equally marked in the life.

Of course, the Bible outranks all other books, and so should be made prominent and pre-eminent. Let the reader remember that when he prays he is talking to God, but when he reads the Bible, God is talking to him. Great is this difference, and few have appreciated it.

A much praised, but a much neglected book is the Bible. And yet it is God talking to us.

It is the soul's book. Other books tell of art, science, law, commerce, etc., but this book tells us about an invisible soul and its invisible home. It deals in spiritual things and tells us how to live spiritually and become fit to see God and live in a spiritual world.

It takes the Holy Spirit to unlock the book. He who reads simply with the eye of the Intellect will miss the glory of the book, and never realize the soul-food with which it is stored. It is well to ask the light and blessing of the Holy Ghost upon us each time that we read.

It is well not only to read prayerfully, but slowly and meditatively as we proceed. The careless and hasty reader will get no benefit. To pass food through a man hurriedly encased in a tin tube will give him no strength; and so a skimming over the Book or a shooting through the mind hastily of certain passages, more as a salve to conscience than anything else, will never give the spiritual life and vigor that is needed. How can it? A salve is not food. Food has to be masticated, digested, assimilated, to become blood, strength and life. So with the Word.

Muller advises the taking of ten or twelve rich verses in the Gospels or Psalms, and reading each verse over slowly four or five times before proceeding to the next. He says the effect will be blessed. Let the reader try it

Fletcher had a way of kneeling down before the Bible with a finger upon a passage, crying out, "Light, Lord." And he always got it. Let the reader try it.

For over a dozen years the writer has read the Bible on his knees. He reads the entire volume through in that way once each year, and the New Testament oftener. It has been a great blessing to him. If the reader is so moved of God let him try it.

Anyhow, let us all pay attention to reading, avoiding every kind of literature that is hurtful to the soul, perusing no book that we would not like Christ to sit down and study with us, selecting the purest and best of religious volumes for our devotional reading, and above all taking the Word of God as the man of our counsel and constant companion.

CHAPTER X.

WITNESSING.

GOD is going to take this world for His Son. There is no question about the final success, no matter how long may be the delay through the sluggishness of His people, and opposition of men and devils.

What method will God use to bring the nations to His feet? It will not be physical force, for the reason that He deals with spirits who are free moral agents and can not be driven. One reason that the Flood was sent, and the fires of wrath swept Sodom and Gomorrah from the face of the earth, was to show men that physical agencies and forces could not reform men. Sin still raged after these judgments, and the same sin at that. Neither were angels sent to preach the Gospel. Men would be paralyzed at the presence of supernatural beings, and could not listen. Neither did God have the message of mercy and life written in blazing letters across the sky, for the people would soon cease to read it, and be as indifferent as they were to the presence of God on Mt. Sinai. Nor does God trust to good literature to bring it about. He could have dropped books and papers on the earth like manna. But men could refuse to read. They could close the books or walk away from them. It is one thing to bring a horse to water, another to make him drink.

God's plan is laid down both in the Old and New Testaments. In the former He says, "Ye are my witnesses." In the latter, "Ye shall be witnesses unto me in Jerusalem, Judea, Samaria and unto the uttermost part of the earth." When a new nation or kingdom arises it at once adopts a flag and weapons. So the morning of Pentecost when the setting up of Christ's kingdom took place, the weapon of conquest was seen resting upon the heads of the one hundred and twenty disciples, in the form of a cloven tongue of fire. It is with this that God proposes to overcome the world,— the tongue. But according to the Scripture it is not an ordinary tongue, but a new tongue, a tongue of fire, a tongue in motion. Just as a flame is seen to have a flickering motion when burning, so must it be with this instrument of God, which He selects to spread the truth —it must not be cold or motionless. And finally it was cloven or split down the middle to show that the man is to talk twice as much as he ever did before. In a word, we are to be witnesses.

God's method is first to fill the man with the facts of salvation and then send the baptism of fire upon him. Sometimes men fail to see the beauty and necessity of this order. All of us have met with men who had the facts but not the fire, and others who had the fire, but not the facts. God's order is facts and fire. He does not want them separated. They make a most wonderful and powerful combination.

So a witness for God after this order is better than a book, no matter how good it is. God's best book of Christian evidence is five or six feet long, eighteen inches broad and bound in human skin. Men can run away from the books that men publish, but God's human book has legs and goes after people. Men's books when closed and unused are powerless, but this book of God, a human teacher, will not be shut up, but pursues one with prayer, testimony and exhortation, until there is nothing left for the pursued to do but to surrender.

This witnessing can of course be more or less efficacious. Some is just what God wants it to be, some could be improved, and some really does harm. We are not only to be witnesses, but a certain kind of witnesses. The Scripture gives hints and directions that if carried out will add immeasurably to our effectiveness. We glance at a few points.

First, we are to witness to the truth. There is no necessity of shunning the truth; we have plenty of facts. As for falsehood, whether it appears in the statement of doctrine or experience, the Spirit of God will not fall upon it. God will not smile upon a lie. It is the truth He wants, and nothing but the truth. We have all lamented that error has been lifted up in pulpits and from the pew. We all know what it is to hear men claiming for themselves in experience what the hollow accent of the voice, the dull leathery look of the face and the unspirituality of the life contradicted. While upon the plain statement of Gospel facts and the simple relation of a genuine experience, the presence of God and the benediction of Heaven are at once felt.

Second, we must witness to the whole truth. Why tell a part and keep back another? If one person has gone deeper in the grace of God than another, why not speak of the greater blessing? If one has made spiritual discoveries, why not proclaim them? If neglected and lost doctrines are recovered, with their consequent experiences, why should we not testify to the enlargement and enrichment of our souls? Does God do what He condemned as absurd in human life, and light a candle to put in under a bushel?

So far from this He says what we hear in the ear that proclaim upon the housetops. And Paul says if the trumpet give an uncertain sound who will prepare himself for the battle, and adds that a stranger coming into our meetings and hearing us declare the facts of grace will fall on his face and say God is with you of a truth.

The very word witness brings guidance here. A witness in the courts is expected to tell all he knows. We are God's witnesses. The Saviour and His power to save is on trial before the bar of the world. We owe it to Him to tell all we know.

It is well to recollect that the knowledge of God is to be spread through the earth by human agencies, and this understanding of the Divine Being and His power to save has thus far kept pace with the utterances of consecrated lips. God is known as men declare Him. A silent church means a spiritually dead community. A testifying Christianity invariably brings the knowledge of God to the people, and great works of grace follow as a consequence. A talking Luther and preaching Wesley brought about two of the greatest revivals of the world. They brought out through faithful witnesses that God could pardon and sanctify, and lo, multitudes accept both of these graces. It was noticed when the cholera was devastating Europe that it advanced in its deadly march about twenty miles a day. This fact led to the discovery that the disease was not atmospheric but contagious, and had to be carried about by people. This twenty miles a day was about the ordinary journey of men at that time. So the Gospel keeps pace with the advance of men. It goes as far as men carry it with their tongues.

This being true for one doctrine is true for all. God does not restore a lost truth and experience by dropping a book from the skies, but through the instrumentality of men filled with the fact and set on fire by the Holy Ghost. So we all owe it to God and to the world in which we live to tell all we know of Christ and His saving power. We should witness to the whole truth. By each one declaring what he has received from God, and what he knows of Him, we will finally clear away spiritual ignorance, and God and His Christ will be sought and blessedly known.

We once listened to a preacher at an annual conference preach a masterly sermon. He had recently received the blessing of sanctification, and the text in a culminating way led him right up to it. As he neared the generally unknown, unexperienced and agitating subject, you could have heard a pin drop. Preachers who had or had not the blessing bent forward for the final explanation, application and direct meaning of the passage. To the astonishment of all, he with every sign of wanting to do his duty, became terrorized, listened to Satan and wheeled off in his remarks in another direction.

A lady approached a world-wide evangelist who claimed to have received the baptism of the Holy Ghost and asked him why he did not preach it. His reply was that the people were not ready for it. This answer was simply amazing as a piece of spiritual pride and ignorance. By this speech he virtually said God had given him a blessing that other people could not have. Was this not pride? As for the ignorance, Peter said: "The promise is to you and to your children, and to them that are afar off and to as many as the Lord our God shall call." The same Bible tells us that God has called us all to holiness. And Paul says that Christ "suffered outside the gate that He might sanctify the *people*."

Third, we are to witness fearlessly. A frightened looking witness on the stand in the court would not make a favorable impression. And so the timid testifier to this great blessing will not do much to the spread of the doctrine. The evident dread of men and fear of remark and opposition will be felt by on-lookers as incongruous and irreconcilable with the possession of a blessing which is claimed to cast out all fear.

We have marvelled at the exhibition of this man-dread at Conferences, Love Feasts and at the home class-meeting. Terms that are Scriptural and Wesleyan, which had been bravely used at the time of the reception of sanctification, and when surrounded by sympathizers and believers in the doctrine, were discarded in an unfriendly atmosphere, and expressions descriptive of religious experience were used so general in their nature as to mean anything or nothing. These kind of people do more damage to the cause than evil spirits from the under world.

It is the calm, earnest and fearless utterance or testimony to a second work of grace that God honors, and that plants a conviction which men find impossible or exceedingly difficult to remove.

Fourth, we must witness in love. This is perfectly reconcilable with the foregoing thought. It is a great mistake to think that courage is the same as pugnaciousness and offensiveness. It does not mean impertinence and rudeness. A man does not walk around with a chip on his shoulder aching for a fight. It does not make a John Sullivan out of a Christian.

> "The bravest are the tenderest,
> The loving are the daring."

The Saviour had no fear of men or devils in his heart, and yet who was so gentle and kind?

The person who thinks He can advance the cause of Christ and holiness by a fierce, defiant and blustering manner will find himself sorely mistaken. It is certainly most desirable to witness to Perfect Love in perfect love. Such a testimony joined to so lovely a spirit becomes irresistible.

While we are called to warn and rebuke, yet we are told to do so "with all longsuffering." Some people seem only happy when they are excoriating others with their speeches. Some one says about them that they "make the promises of God too hot to hold."

We are not asking for a "sickening sweetness" of life. We are pleading for a spirit of love as we witness for God and sanctification. We want "honey out of the rock." That is a sweet, loving spirit out of a firm, consistent life. The life can be like a rock for steadfastness, while love flows from it like honey.

It is wonderful how people will listen to us if they feel we really love them. It is marvelous what rebukes they will stand if they hear the accent of kindness and love in the voice.

We once wondered how the great multitudes stood the abusive language of a certain national evangelist. There in cold print were the most offensive terms, and yet the multitudes hung upon his words and turned by hundreds to the Lord. When at last we heard the man for ourself the whole thing was explained. We found his face shone with the light of good humor and a genuine love for sinners, and when the expressions were used that if spoken in real harshness would have maddened the crowd, we found they were uttered in such a smiling and loving way that resentment was completely disarmed.

We do not hold up all of this case as a model, but to illustrate how necessary in our witnessing that we should be full of love.

Fifth, we must witness in the power of the Holy Ghost.

It is remarkable how trying and irritating religious testimony is that comes merely from the lips and throat. All of us know the weariness, dreariness and general tinpanniness of a witnessing that is without unction. It sounds as if memorized, is parrot-like, juiceless and powerless.

The effective testifying is from the Spirit-filled heart. The individual may not be in an ecstasy, but the abiding presence of the Holy Spirit in the soul will give a thrill, life and force to the words uttered, no matter how simple they are, that will never fail to do good.

It is remarkable that witnessing is connected by Christ with the Baptism of the Holy Ghost or the second work of grace. He said to the disciples, "Ye shall receive power after that the Holy Ghost is come upon you ; and ye shall be witnesses unto me both in Jerusalem, and in all Judea, and in Samaria, and unto the uttermost part of the earth."

The difficulty realized in getting regenerated people to testify, and the readiness and volubility of sanctified people on the witness stand, are here both made perfectly plain by the words of the Saviour just quoted.

Let us see to it that we always speak in the Spirit and by the Spirit. What a freshness, spiritual beauty and tender power is felt to reside in the simple, honest utterances of such followers of God.

Still, we are not to keep silence simply because there may be no conscious afflatus or mighty spiritual exaltation. Oftentimes most gracious blessings will come to the soul when speaking out for God in times of heaviness through peculiar besetments and temptations. And furthermore, it is well to remember that the testimony of every one who lives right will be honored of God, whether he has religious raptures at the time or not.

Sixth, we are called not to be lawyers for God, but witnesses.

Many make a profound mistake here. They feel that God expects them to make masterly arguments for Him in proof of this "secret of the Lord," this "mystery of the Gospel," this blessed doctrine of entire sanctification.

They overlook the fact that a secret is not found out by arguments, but has to be revealed. A mystery does not succumb to syllogisms. Men can not be reasoned into sanctification. God has not sent out a set of ecclesiastical lawyers and arguers to settle these grave questions, but a band of witnesses.

We have observed in the courts of law that witnesses are not expected to argue and plead, but to tell what they know. This is what God expects of His people. Tell what you know about Him. It is testimony concerning actual knowledge and experience, and not fine orations, that bows down the human heart and sweeps souls to Christ.

Many have overlooked the plain statement of the Bible that we are simply witnesses. Feeling that they had no special gifts; that they did not know how to defend the truth skillfully; that they were not eloquent and wise; they have set back in idleness and unprofitableness, when all God wanted was their testimony.

A witness tells what he knows, and so in the

courts can be a child or a very ignorant person. It is not learning or eloquence the court is after, but facts, and the facts with which the witness is familiar.

This is what God expects of us. Not a harangue of the hustings, not misty speculation, not golden worded orations, but a loving, faithful, tireless declaration of what we know about Jesus and His power to make holy and keep holy.

The world is anxious for argument. They are willing to dispute. But it would have been a mistake for Heaven to have sent us out to confront the world on its strong side, and that too, when so many of God's people are illiterate and could be easily wound up argumentatively by a skillful master of debate on the other side. Instead of this, God institutes a flank attack on the world, and sends against its reasoners a band of shining-faced, happy-souled people who, with an overflowing gladness, are irresistible and unanswerable in Spirit-empowered and fire-baptized utterances of what they feel and know in Divine things.

The writer once held a meeting in one of our Southern States. A certain member of the church in the town at once put himself in opposition to the doctrine that was preached and to all done at the services. To his astonishment and chagrin first his wife and next his son, who was a young man, obtained the blessing of sanctification. At once he sought to bring them into an argument, and so goaded them with stinging remarks and bantered them for a forensic contest. But the wife was a sensible woman and seemed to take intuitively the proper course under the circumstances. When the husband followed her into the kitchen where she was supervising the preparation of breakfast or dinner, and tried to get her to dispute about the holy experience, she however would not thus be betrayed, and simply replied, "I have it, husband," and went on silently with her work. The defeated and exasperated man went into the garden, where his son was digging among the vegetables, and tried in like manner to arouse him, but he being taught of his mother made no reply. By this time the husband and father was filled with such anguish that he wanted to scream. He went into his parlor and rolled on the floor and pulled his hair. He admitted it all some days after. No one would argue with him, and he was miserable. He was steadily being whipped out by gentle replies and silence. In a week's time he went down, not by the reasoning of a lawyer in the kingdom, but by the gentle, discreet speech of two of God's witnesses.

Seventh, the testimony and the life of the witnesses should agree.

It is wonderful what an added power is given to Christian testimony when the spirit, conversation, conduct and, in a word, the life harmonizes with the profession. On the other hand, the soul of the listener fairly sickens in hearkening to the relation of high and holy experiences, when the daily walk and actions of the man will not bear it out. The very voice of the speaker is against him. Spiritual hollowness is heard. There is much apparent fervor of speech, even frenzy of manner, but that indescribable unction that comes from the Holy One is absent. So men listen and behold, with crawly sensations running along the nerves, and inward spiritual distress that is not unlike nausea.

The professor must be a possessor. We must live what we witness to. When we do this God smiles and men are moved.

This harmony and agreement of speech and life is brought out in the Old Testament in the robe of the high priest. On the border of the garment were golden bells and pomegranates. There were twelve of each, and the order was a bell and a pomegranate, a bell and a pomegranate unto the end. The voice from this remarkable fringe should make us all thoughtful. The bells stood for testimony and the pomegranates for the fruits of the life. And the parable was that the testimony and life equal each other. Ring out the bells of Christian witnessing, but let the fruits of the life measure up exactly to the testimony.

Some would destroy the beautiful truth thus taught of God, and so alter the numbers that had been commanded by the Lord. Some believe in six bells and eighteen pomegranates; that is, they want the life to be ahead of the testimony. They fail to read the lesson on the fringe. Others believe in six pomegranates and eighteen bells. They talk more than they possess. God's reply to both of these mistaken individuals is seen in the skirt of the robe—twelve bells and twelve pomegranates. Let word and act agree, let lip and performance or witness and life measure up exactly the same.

These seven features are the marks and guiding posts for that difficult thing—a true and faithful witnessing for holiness. If we observe them we shall do well.

Of course, there will be opposition to this plan of God for taking the world. What divine plan and work is not opposed? This has ever been seen and will be witnessed until the Great Rebellion of the Universe shall be put down, and men's lives flow into channels of the divine will.

Satan will naturally oppose a plan that has succeeded so well, and is destined to bring the nations to the knowledge of the truth. Fearing the life and flaming witness, he would stifle utterance, lock the jaws of God's people and fill them with dumb devils. How Christ used to love to cast them out! "I charge thee, thou dumb spirit, . . come out of him." And he had to come!

The world opposes the plan, while recognizing its

wisdom and adopting it as a method of pushing and increasing its own vast business and colossal fortunes. The merchant who fills one of his agents with facts about the trade and fires him with the prospect of a larger salary and possible partnership, does identically what Christ has already done, and yet fails to see his own inconsistency.

A formal church opposes the divine plan, because to a cold, stiff ecclesiasticism a joyous, ringing testimony is unpalatable and offensive. It would be hard to describe the pain endured by such a body of people when suddenly brought face to face with a demonstrative type of piety, and compelled to listen to clear-cut religious experiences of happy and triumphant character. Such things are not desired in many places. Graveyards as a rule are very quiet.

The backslider is against the divine plan. The reason is easily fathomed. There is no kind of speech that is more painful, that will more quickly bring misery and condemnation to the spiritually lapsed man than the bright, joyous witnessing of God's sanctified people. It cuts deeper than a Damascus blade. It reminds the faithless one of departed joys and glory. It is a picture of what he himself used to be. So, as the merry carolling of birds is a torture to a miserable man, so the wretchedness of the backslider is intensified in listening to the joyful and victorious experience of his unfallen brother.

So, in view of all these opposing forces we may look for an array of reasons urged by the opposition, as to why we should be silent, while they in great apparent friendliness tell us to keep our counsel, to say less and do more, live what we have, possess but do not profess, etc., etc., etc.

There is not an argument which they thus use against the testifying to sanctification but could be promptly urged against regeneration or any other of the Christian doctrines, and indeed Christianity itself.

A prominent man in our church said that as soon as he heard a man say he was sanctified, he doubted it at once, on the principle that he would question a person's truth in his mind when he went around claiming to be honest. How strange it was that the wide difference of the two speeches did not impress him. One being a boasting of self, the other a glorying of a work of God.

From this and all other confusing speeches of opposition we must turn to God's Word both in the Old and New Testaments, where we are told that we are to be witnesses. As such we are to press on the divinely appointed way, whether men smile or frown, meet us with garlands or greet us with stones.

The failure to carry out God's plan in regard to a clear-cut testimony of what He has done to us and is now to us, is certain to bring spiritual darkness and calamity. Very long and sorrowful indeed is the list of preachers and laymen, men and women, who possessed the blessing of sanctification, hid the talent in a napkin, tried to live the experience, toned it down in various ways to suit family, friends and church, until at last they awoke to see the star had disappeared, the angels had vanished into the skies, and the glory had departed.

If we follow faithfully the divine plan of witnessing, not only with the life but the lips, certain gracious and blessed results will be felt at once to arise and increase as the days go by.

One will be a sense of increased light and gladness with every occasion of witnessing. Each time the duty is performed the Spirit will smile upon the soul well pleased

Another result will be a growing freedom or sense of religious liberty.

A third effect will be a consciously increasing strength.

A fourth wlll be the arousing of conviction on the subject all about you. The testimony may be modestly and simply given, but if uttered clearly and unctiously it will never fail, but hearts will be stirred, and souls set to panting after this great grace of God. The song will reach the heart, the arrow will strike the mark, the testimony in a word will never fall to the ground. God will take care of it.

What was once said by an aged sanctified lady at

a large camp ground was never forgotten by a young preacher who heard her that morning, but prepared the way for the blessing which he received years afterward. Many hundreds of such instances could be related.

A fifth result is that contemplated by the Lord in the spread of His truth and knowledge over the world, and the nations brought to live at His feet.

In Jerusalem the Latins and Greeks have a custom annually of obtaining what they call Holy Fire from the reputed sepulchre of our Lord. For hours they in great crowds watch the orifice from which they expect the outbursting flame. At last, when thousands are keyed to the highest pitch of expectancy, the flame is seen darting out of the crevice of the tomb, when with great shouts and cries the people rush toward it with tapers, candles, torches, and crowding and falling over one another, try to ignite what they bear in their hands. As soon as this is done they rush away in every direction, some on foot, others on horseback, waving their flambeaux and multiplying their lights an hundred and a thousand fold as others come in touch with them; so that in the course of a few hours the landscape is dotted with myriads of twinkling fires, the country looks as if a glittering firmament had fallen upon it, and the Holy Fire is scattered everywhere.

So we are to take fire under Christ, and burn all

the more brightly as we run; and we are to scatter the fire as we go, preaching, teaching, praying, singing, shouting and testifying. Sparks from us should kindle others. We should have flame enough in our own souls and tongues to set every cold church and dead community blazing all over the land. Fire ought to fall as we preach, and scatter as we witness. Through us extinguished human torches should flame again, and new lives glow that never burned before. As we go through life thus faithful to Christ the fire will fall, and as it comes down on us it will spread through us to individuals, homes, neighborhoods, cities and countries. Long lines of enkindled men and women will move across the world in every direction, igniting millions of others, until at last the darkness will be driven away through an army of heavenly torch-bearers, a heavenly firmament of truth will be seen scintillating and sparkling down on the face of the earth and God's holy fire will be flaming everywhere.

CHAPTER XI.

GOOD WORKS.

PAUL tells us to be "careful to maintain good works." They are not simply advisable but essential in several important particulars. Salvation comes by faith alone, but salvation will not remain if we neglect good works. The experience of sanctification does not put us where we do not need to discharge them. This would be akin to antinomianism. It is incumbent on the sanctified man to maintain good works, if he would retain a clear and gracious experience.

What are good works? They are not necessarily church works. There is a difference, and in many instances a very great difference. In a certain sense church works are necessary, and in them we find most excellent people actively engaged.

By church works we mean building and repairing; carpeting, cushioning and ornamenting the house of God, purchasing a larger organ, elevating the spire, bronzing the doors, staining the windows, and doing many other like things too numerous to mention.

It is evident to any one that, while some of these

things are necessary and excellent in their way, yet they could not be called spiritual works. Unconverted people without a particle of grace in their souls could easily perform them. Indeed, all of us have known men and women prominent in this kind of work, who showed by their spirit, conversation and life, that they knew not God, and possessed not the mind or salvation of Christ.

We are not commanded to do these things in the Bible, for the same reason perhaps, that we are not ordered to feed and clothe ourselves. We need no urging to build ourselves houses, and after that beautiful church homes.

On the other hand, Good Works are enjoined frequently. Great stress is laid upon them, for it is made clear in the Scriptures that much depends on their performance. To crown all, they alone are mentioned at the Day of Judgment. Let the reader turn to Matt. xxv. and get some idea of what works are good and worthy of reward in the estimation of the Son of God. Certainly they must be important when after the world is burned up and Time has ended these are the only things mentioned before the Throne.

Think of it! the only things. Listen to what they are—feeding the hungry, giving water to the thirsty, clothing the naked, remembering the stranger, visiting the sick, and going to the prisoner.

Not a word about great military exploits and statesmanlike deeds! Not a single allusion to that kind of public greatness so dear to the hearts of many! Not even a word about the building of churches and all the performances known as church work.

Suppose the words of the Judge at that day were: "Well done; for ye built a beautiful church with a lofty spire and pealing organ. Ye gave great entertainments and floored the church with brussel carpets, stained the windows with gorgeous colors, and made them resplendent with the figures of the saints." If such were the words uttered, how many unconverted and unspiritual members of the church would stand honored, crowned and rewarded at the Judgment. But no such words will be heard. And first for the reason that these are simply church works. Next, that instead of being Good Works, they can be discharged from sheer selfish motives. It is an instinct with a bird to make its nest as soft and pleasant as possible. The very pig in the sty roots up the mud to make a bed comfortable and satisfactory to himself. And cushioned pews and carpeted aisles may be nothing more in the sight of God than what we see done by the animal, save as the man can work with greater elegance and more artistic finish than a pig.

One thing is certain, that the Lord knew there was no need to command people to make beautiful and comfortable churches. This they would do for their own comfort. It is a physical pleasure to worship in a nicely furnished church edifice. In addition to the selfish instinct we can also see that ecclesiastical pride may be at the bottom of much that is called church work. The tapering spire may be built to tower above the belfry of a sister denomination. The deep-toned organ may be purchased with a secret pleasure that it out-thunders the choir of another church. So it is readily seen why none of these things are mentioned as a cause of approval and reward at the Judgment. Church works are not necessarily Good Works.

Let it not be supposed that we do not believe in handsome temples of worship for God, and in the doing of all those things in the line of glass, paint and carpet to keep up the material side of the visible kingdom of God. We mean to say that these works can be performed by unconverted people, can be done with God thrust out of the heart and life, and from motives that instead of pleasing would be highly offensive to Heaven. These may, in a sense, be called Good Works, but they are not those that are mentioned before the Throne. Happy the man who can abound in both, but if we had to select we would choose the deeply spiritual labor rather than that kind of work which can be performed by worldly hearted members of the church. We would far rather help the poor than pay for stained glass or a memorial window.

It is well to remember that the Bible Good Works

of feeding the poor, visiting the sick and prisoners have their spiritual side. God knew, and we all know, that the person who does these things will not forget or neglect the soul. It now becomes necessary to show the superiority of Good Works, and why they alone are mentioned in the Great Day of Rewards.

One thing about them is that they prove our faith. James says distinctly that our faith without works is dead. Of course, he referred to Good Works. That church works do not prove faith will be readily admitted. All of us who have seen unconverted people help in this line of labor will quickly admit that. The writer has known the most thoroughly worldly people prominent in what is called church work. Any preacher knows that this kind of fussy activity and spirituality are not synonymous. Such things do not prove that Christ is living in one. But let a person be seen visiting the sick, going to pray with prisoners, and relieving the necessity of the suffering, and such a life declares the genuine faith.

Again Good Works convict the world. None of us ever knew of a sinner smiting his breast and saying, "God be merciful to me a sinner," because some man painted a church or carpeted the floor. But it is marvelous how the sight of a man feeding the hungry, clothing the naked, visiting the sick and exercising hospitality to the stranger will convince the mind and move the heart of the most careless, concerning the facts and truth of the Gospel of the Son of God. Somehow such a life convicts. One reason may be is that it reminds one so much of Christ. The Man of Galilee is projected before us again doing good.

Still again Good Works bless the world. We might multiply church steeples and organs, stain every window and paint every rectory and parsonage, but the world's suffering and heart-brokenness would be just the same. Such things do not put bread in starving mouths or wipe tears from overflowing eyes. Perhaps there is an added bitterness to the pang of the ragged, starving wretch, as he glances at some of our elegant sanctuaries, where the bronzed doors alone cost enough to satisfy the hunger and clothe the shivering bodies of many thousands. Lonely, homeless, friendless, the poorly dressed and desperate man hardly feels that he would be welcome in some of our luxurious abodes of worship. So he slinks by the marble stepped entrance into the cold dark street beyond, the very inscription in the guarded vestibule, "Come ye yourselves apart and rest awhile," reading like a mockery.

On the other hand, it is impossible to do the things that Christ mentions at the Judgment without benefitting, cheering and blessing mankind. Bread and clothing given mean hunger and cold removed; visiting the sick means sympathy, consolation, and heart burdens rolled away; while coming to the prisoner is not only the lighting up of a dreary cell but oftentimes the salvation of a despairing soul.

Again, Good Works bless the worker. It is wonderful how the soul can remain narrow, cold and undeveloped in simple church work. But we challenge any one to do the six things mentioned by Christ as Good Works without feeling the heart put in a flame and the spiritual nature sweeten, expand and become more and more Christ-like with a rapidity that will not only astonish the person himself, but those who look upon him.

We read once of a member of a church who had been careless in regard to this kind of spiritual activity. He had a habit of fretting and fault-finding. He saw very little good in anything, was skeptical in regard to the sincerity of bright testimonies which he heard in experience meetings, and was greatly given to arguing about non-essentials. One Sunday morning his pastor preached on Heaven. Immediately the combative, skeptical spirit arose and he said: "You speak of heaven, but can you give me any idea as to the location, whether in the center of the universe or close by us in our own solar system?"

The pastor replied: "I will give you my views at another time. Let me now speak to you about something else. Do you see yonder little house on the hill?"

"Yes," replied the man.

"Well, in there lives a woman, poor, sick and helpless. She needs coal, food and consolation. I wish you could drop in a few minutes some time and see her."

That very afternoon this gentleman, who was a man of some means, went to the little house. With him he had brought certain things in the shape of fuel and provisions. He sat an half hour by the side of the invalid, read a chapter in God's Word, sung a hymn, and kneeling down prayed with her. On leaving he placed a five dollar bill in her hand. The next day he met his pastor on the street and calling him aside said:

"I asked you yesterday where heaven was. You need not tell me. I have found out. Do you see that little house on the hill? Well, it is there! I found it there yesterday afternoon as I talked and prayed with a sick woman; and it is also in my heart."

We remember to have read of a Christian who was once active and happy in the service of God. For some reason he discontinued his Good Works, and soon after became a prey to gloomy and despondent reflections. After a farther lapse of time he became morose, bitter, wished to die, and one day while sitting alone before the fire in his room determined to kill himself. He concluded to die by hanging, and so went down the street and purchased a small rope for the ghastly deed. He placed the rope in his overcoat pocket, and was so anxious to expedite matters that he took a near cut back to his hotel along a narrow street lined with wretched-looking tenement houses, a route he never remembered to have gone before. As he was passing one of the most poverty-stricken of all the dwellings, a cry of such misery and despair came through a window that he stopped, and hearing it repeated walked into the hall, and from thence through an open door into a room, where his eyes beheld as much wretchedness to the square yard as he had ever seen, read or heard of before. A man had just breathed his last on a miserable pallet of straw in the corner. He looked as if he might have died from starvation. A woman with the same starved look hung over him with the desolate cry that had been heard. The room had nothing in it save the straw pallet, a crazy-looking chair and table and a box in the corner in which two children were huddled to keep warm. There was no covering on the floor, nor curtains to the windows, nor fire in the empty grate. The cold wind was blowing at a great rate through a broken window pane. The woman looked sick and pale, while the children ragged, cold and hungry, filled the eyes with tears at the first sight.

Our friend with the suicidal intent only paused a moment to take in the mournful scene, and darted out on benevolent mission. In a few minutes he had a fire burning cheerily in the grate, and food abundant smoking on the table. He had the dead cared for, and a good bed brought in for the living. In a short while he had physician and nurse, for he was a man of means, and purchased other things that were needed for health and comfort. As he surveyed the changed room, the children eating before the comfortable fire the metamorphosis was great. And all this pleasing change had been effected by a servant of God with a little money.

He had bought a large blanket to hang up before the window to keep out the chilly blast, and his last act before leaving was to hang it in place. Finding some difficulty in doing this, he felt in his overcoat pocket and found a rope. Immediately he tied the corners of the blanket with it and hung the piece of goods then easily and successfully. After this he left the room and house, and pursued his way to his room. As he sat before the fire meditating there was a sweet, happy feeling warming his heart that he had not felt for months. But suddenly remembering that he was going to hang himself he put his hand into his coat pocket for the rope and lo, it was gone! At once he recalled that he had tied it to the blanket in the tenement house. But this was not all the surprise, for on looking into his heart he found now that he did not want to die. Thus once more in the work of doing good he had tasted the real sweetness of life, and knew now why he ought to live, and above all how to live.

So, he did not die, but lived. We repeat it with great emphasis and significance—he lived!

Fifth. Good Works comfort us in a dying hour. All of us will have to die. When that trying moment comes, we may be sure that the thought which will be sweetest will be the recollection of the good we have done in the name and in the spirit of Jesus. As Jennie Deane said to the Queen of England as she plead for her sister's life: "Ah, madam, when we come to die, it is not what we have done for ourselves, but what we have done for others that we love to think of most pleasantly."

Happy is the man who, propped up on a dying pillow, can look down a long line of men and women whom he has fed, clothed, warmed, cheered and helped in different ways. May we all have such glad memories at that trying hour.

It is said that during the Crimean War a Russian officer was patrolling the lines on a bitterly cold night, when he came across a sentinel thinly clad and almost freezing in the piercing blast. At once the officer took off his overcoat and wrapped it about the soldier. Next day there was a terrible battle and many thousands were killed and wounded. Among the latter was the young officer whose life blood was fast gushing away on the bare ground and under a bleak sky. Friends were bending over him as he rambled unconsciously in his mind. Suddenly he opened his eyes and looking upward gasped in glad accents:

"The Saviour is coming for me."

There was a moment's silence as he still gazed steadily upward, when with a look of astonishment and a great light flashing over his face and a strange, sweet smile on his lips he cried:

"Why he has the overcoat on I gave to the soldier."

In another moment the noble spirit was gone, but what an inexpressibly, beautiful truth was left us, that Christ comes to us in the moment of death clothed with the Good Works we have done in His name.

Sixth. Good Works will affect our reward in heaven. Through faith we obtain a title and entrance into heaven, but our Works, the Good Works that are the fruit of a saving faith, settle the fact of our moral grade and position in the world of glory. Paul says in Corinthians that those whose works are of such a character that they shall be burned up, that they will be saved as by fire, but will themselves suffer loss. And here is the loss, not of heaven itself, for he says they will be saved though as by fire. The loss will be seen in reward, for the Bible says, "Every man shall be rewarded according to his *works*."

A mere glance at the glorified bodies of the redeemed will show what each one did for God on earth.

As one star differeth from another star in glory so also shall be the resurrection of the dead. There will be no need for a trumpet-like proclamation that the universe may know what men and women achieved and suffered for Christ. The flashing crown, lustrous body, superior authority, the rule over ten cities instead of five or one; these and other things as unmistakable will be the heavenly language or method of declaring how we have endured, and conquered, and what we have done and become for God

CHAPTER XII.

FASTING—TITHES—AND DRESS.

IN Ezekiel's prophecy of the great coming blessing of holiness to the church, he gives us some striking marks and characteristics of the people of God under the transforming grace of that time.

He says among other things that they will "walk in my statutes," and "keep my judgments and do them." In other words, they will rigidly and faithfully obey the commandments of God.

It is remarkable how careless God's regenerated children are in regard to some of the divine statutes. We do not mean that they live criminally or go into gross sin, and yet there are some "statutes" they do not observe as they should. When first converted they were careful to keep all; how tender was the conscience, how careful to please Heaven at every step, and in little things as well as great things. But after a few months or years there comes the letting down, and the talk of "freedom," and becoming "broader," etc. The Sabbath was kept holy for months after their conversion, and then by and by the tender feeling that it is "The Lord's Day" seems to pass away and we see in letter writing, social visits, carriage drives, and car travel that it is no longer "holy," as it used to be. Some even go to their stores to write business letters or straighten up shelves, some go to the Post-office for mail, and certain articles are purchased on the Sabbath without a pang of conscience, when the time was that it could not be done.

This one instance is given to show what we mean by God's children becoming careless about keeping His statutes.

It is so blessed to feel that God has a blessing or work of grace for His people which when it comes upon them will perpetuate the tenderness and quickened spiritual sensibility received at the time of regeneration. That when the Lord takes the "stone out of the heart," and "puts His Spirit in us," that then as Ezekiel says, God's servants, now purified, fired, filled and established, will "walk in His statutes," and "keep His judgments and do them." It brings the soul into a life of perpetual faithfulness. There will be no let-down as long as the grace itself is kept.

ot only will the commandments be faithfully kept, but statutes and teachings of the Kingdom that are regarded as secondary and less important, and often overlooked by the regenerated or carelessly dropped, will be faithfully observed by the truly sanctified. One of these is

FASTING.

It is remarkable how few Christians practice this

means of grace. It has become burdensome. It was too great a trial to the flesh. It was a painful blow aimed at the kitchen god. So the weekly fast was changed into a quarterly meeting means of grace, then finally discontinued altogether. The plea of physical weakness and a sick headache was made. Ultimately the argument was urged of having becoming "freer" and "broader." And so the fast day ceased.

All this is done in the face of the fact that fasting is enjoined in the Scriptures; that the prophets fasted, that Jesus Christ fasted, and that He said some things would not come out except by fasting and prayer. In His Sermon on the Mount He tells how to do when we fast that we might not appear unto men to fast. The Pharisees were not condemned for fasting, but for doing it in a way to obtain human notice and praise. Like all of God's statutes, it brings benefit to the physical man as well as to the soul. To fast once a week is a benediction to the body, a help to the mind as well as grace to the soul.

We do not mean that one should go without food for twenty-four hours. This we believe would in many cases produce sickness or a condition of helplessness. God does not want us to unfit ourselves for home duties and His service. The sacrifice of a single meal once a week can be gone through with by most Christians, not only without injury to body or work, but will bring a blessing to soul, body and work.

In case that the constitution is so feeble or peculiar that even a single meal can not be given up, then let abstinence be practiced, that is, some favorite dish be refrained from at a certain time.

We repeat, that many Christians have given up fasting, but we know a certain body of sanctified people all over the United States who are as regular to observe Friday morning as a fast day as they remember the Sabbath to go to worship. They have found out, as Christ said, not only that some things will not come out except by fasting, but also that some things will not come down without this duty.

We have been engaged in meetings where for days people had prayed for the descent of the Spirit and the breaking up time, when it would occur to us to appoint a fast, and lo! on the next day or next service the power would fall, and the altar would be filled with convicted men and women.

The sanctified people have also found out that fasting always brings a blessing to the soul. It may not be felt on the day of self-denial, but it is certain to come on the next with a sense of increased light, strength and peace.

Another duty we would mention is seen in the matter of

TITHES.

This was an ancient religious custom or law, as we see Abraham paying tithes to Melchisedec. It was thoroughly established in the Levitical Economy, and as far as we can see has never been revoked. A liberty peculiar to the Gospel is allowed Christians to increase the amount if desired, while all feel that if the Jew was willing to give his God one-tenth of his substance, surely a Christian should love his Saviour enough not to give *less* than a tenth.

Christianity does not put an end to giving so far as we have studied it in the Gospel and in life. As soon as Zaccheus was saved he gave half of his goods to the poor, while the followers of Christ after the Baptism of the Holy Ghost sold their possessions and laid the money at the apostles' feet for general distribution.

A niggardly sanctified man is an anomaly. We can not but question whether the Baptism of Fire has ever touched his soul as we observe the tight grasp he has upon his pocket-book under the various calls of God.

It has been a question with some as to what is a tenth. Does the Scripture mean a tenth of a man's income, or a tenth of what is left of the annual income after paying all expenses?

This last query is calculated to make one smile, for with many nothing is left after expenses, and it is easy to run the expenses up to take in all the income, and so leave nothing for God.

The truth is that one-tenth of the income should be given to the Lord's cause. One-tenth should be considered a part of one's expenses; only it should be regarded as peculiarly sacred as due the Lord, and hence faithfully paid. For instance, if the income of the farm, store or office, or the salary or wages be one thousand dollars a year, one hundred dollars of that belongs to God. We have no right to let our household expenses go into that sacred tenth.

It is best to keep an account with God in this matter. It will not do to trust to memory, or give spasmodically. The result of doing this way is that God is cheated out of His part, and the religious experience of the brother who abhors rules becomes as fitful as his giving.

There is a double blessing to the Christian who faithfully tithes his money—a spiritual and a temporal blessing. A man need only enter upon the practice to find them both. It makes the soul fair fat and flourishing to give regularly and systematically to God. And He who blessed the land and flocks of the Jews when they honored the Lord with their substance, blesses us just as truly in basket and store to-day for the observance of the same duty.

Recently we heard a sanctified preacher say that for years he has been giving a tenth of all he makes to God, and that as a strange result, which had never been before, he is now never out of money, that he always has some in his purse and in the house. This sounded like an Old Testament echo when the wise man told God's people, "Honor the

Lord with thy substance, and with the first fruits of all thine increase : so shall thy barns be filled with plenty and thy presses shall burst out with new wine." It is true we are not to give to God in order to be materially blessed, but we will be thus blessed nevertheless.

It is the thought of what God has done for us in this world, and the sight of Christ hanging on the cross dying for us, and the contemplation of the blessed and beautiful heaven provided for us that should send a rush of grateful love through every Christian heart and make us only too glad to give to him and thus relieve the burdened soul.

Wesley gave far more than a tenth, and we know others like him who give more than that amount. Let us see to it as sanctified people that we will not give less than a tenth. We will not regret it in this life, nor at the Judgment, nor in heaven.

A third neglected or overlooked duty is seen in

DRESS.

The subject was presented with force by the Spirit at the time of conversion, but from lack of teaching and example the impression wore off, and to-day it is hard to tell the church member from the mere worldling when it comes to a difference in attire.

The Bible is clear in its commands and demands here. The Spirit as well writes these things upon truly awakened and regenerated souls. But people speak of "changed times," and the "nineteenth century," and "freedom" and becoming "broad," and so the Word is ignored and the Spirit is refused a hearing.

The child of God ought not to dress like the child of the world. Reason is against it, conscience is against it, and the Word of God is unmistakable.

For a withering, sarcastic description of the dress of fashion let the reader turn to Isaiah, chapter iii., verses 16–24. We see the same spectacle to-day on our streets.

In I. Timothy, chapter ii., verses 9 and 10, Paul speaks of the question of dress and protests against "braided (or plaited) hair," "gold" "pearls" and "costly array."

In I. Peter, chapter iii., verse 3, Peter condemns the three things of "plaiting the hair," "wearing of gold" and "putting on of apparel," evidently costly apparel.

We certainly have enough Revelation on the subject, and yet to press these duties upon many congregations to-day would be to raise a perfect storm of ridicule and indignation.

We thank God that according to Ezekiel there is a work of grace, which when received by the child of God makes him or her "walk in his statutes" and "do his judgments." To obtain the blessing of sanctification is to regulate at once the dress.

The writer found it impossible to keep a handsome and valuable gold watch ticking in his vest pocket while people are dying for lack of bread through the world, and heathen are without Bibles and preachers to tell them the good news of salvation. He has known many ladies to take the diamonds out of their ears and turn them into missionary money or help therewith a Home for the Fallen.

At this point we can not but recall the story of a prominent woman in the nobility, who gave up from conscientious scruples two valuable diamonds. She had a hospital built with the proceeds for the fallen of her sex. At certain times she visited the wards, and one day was ministering religious comfort to a dying woman in one of the cots. She was sitting by the side of the bed when the dying woman looking up at her said: "Ah, Madam, but for you I would not have had this quiet, home-like place in which to die, and more than that, I would not have been prepared to die. But you taught me here, and you have led me to Jesus, and I am going to Him now through what you have done." Then raising herself up partially, she bent over the hand of her benefactress, and, in imprinting a kiss thereon, let two large crystal tears drop upon it. The next moment she fell back dead upon her pillow.

The lady sat silent and awed a few minutes, looking down at the peaceful face before her, when lifting up her hand she noticed the two tears still glistening upon it. At once a sweet smile flashed over her face and looking upward, she said : "Lord, you have sent me back my two diamonds, and they are so much lovelier and precious than when I gave them to you."

Somehow we feel that Christ could not dress as we have seen some of His servants do in the midst of the physically and spiritually starving millions of earth.

But there is another side to this question. There can be and have been experiences in the dress question that are to be deplored. Poor human nature in reforms is so apt to go as far the opposite way as it had gone in another. Like a milkpan when tilted, at once rushes back as far the other way, so we have seen a like principle at work with people who try to rectify and redeem the past and get right.

We therefore have looked at two extremes in the dress question—fashion's folly and the folly of fanaticism. The extreme of Fashion makes a woman look like an animated show window, and the extreme of Fanaticism makes a female look like a bean pole with a gunny sack wrapped around her. Both are scare-crows,—one gaudy, the other homely.

There is a lovely middle ground somewhere, and it is not the ground of compromise. There is a quiet, tasteful, becoming way of dressing that we believe will be pleasing to God as well as to man.

We do not think that it is for us to tell people that

they must all buy their goods from the same bolt of cloth, and that in the face of all the different ranks and conditions of life. One kind of dress is needed for the factory and another for the store. Nor do we think that any of us have a right to dictate to people how to cut and wear the goods which they in the love and fear of God have purchased for themselves. Some people would make their own taste a law or standard for everybody else, and so cause the whole race to look like a charity school or orphan asylum with the same kind of checked apron on, and hair all combed the same way.

We have a right to protest against rich and extravagant dressing, for the Bible condemns it; but when the people of God are dressing conscientiously we must allow them liberty in many respects, and remember that they have light, as well as the brother and sister with the rigid ascetic and hermitic notions.

A wise man has truly said that the best way to do in this matter is to dress so as not to be conspicuous either way.

The Word of God, the Spirit of God, a good taste and sound common sense will all help us in this disputed question, and bring us to a conclusion that will please God, and satisfy us, although it may not content the self-constituted milliners of the church.

Still the fact remains that to become sanctified will be to have a wonderful change of mind and feeling about dress. And the sweet simplicity of Jesus Christ in us will bring forth something corresponding in our garb and habiliments. Men laugh at Quaker simplicity, but it is notable that in great revivals, when the Spirit of God comes with unobstructed power, that analogous reforms in dress are invariably seen. So with the rise of Methodism, and the later rise of the Salvation Army, the simplicity of dress was beheld each time. Is it not also significant that in times of great spiritual power in religious meetings, that people have been seen by scores tearing finery and valuables from their persons and giving it all to the church that the Gospel might be sent to the dying millions of the heathen world?

As to the character of goods and price of clothing, we must leave these things to the individual conscience of the child of God who is living right, and walking daily with his Saviour. He will guide them and lead them into all truth.

As for the writer, he tries to dress decently and be comingly in clean linen and spotless black. To him it would be a moral impossibility to wear a beaver hat, don a broadcloth suit, carry a gold watch and swing a gold-headed cane. Yet he would not for the world set up his personal taste, and conception of the Bible teaching of the dress question as a law and standard for others. Instead he would say let each person with the Bible before him and Christ in his heart, be fully persuaded in his own mind.

The rule is, do not dress so as to be conspicuous either way. Do not be a fashionable scare-crow for the devil, and do not be a fanatical scare-crow for God. Though of the two we would rather be a scare-crow for God. Let us dress as the Bible teaches and the Spirit directs, and get a tranquil conscience and please God, whether we please anyone else or not.

So to sum up these three overlooked statutes we find that when observed they help to make us "a people."

In fact, Ezekiel declares in connection with what we have been writing about that as a result God says, "Ye shall be my people."

At one time in our lives we wondered why it was so difficult to tell God's people from the world's throng. Oftentimes we have seen great congregations sweeping out of churches into the street, and such was the similarity of dress, manner, bearing, conversation, and all, that we could not tell the Christian from the man of the world.

Is there not a way by which the difference shall be easily manifested? Are there no lines, marks, habits and moral teachings by which the child of God can at once be recognized, and God's people be made to stand forth clear and separate from the world's crowd? It certainly ought to be so, and Ezekiel says it is so. But he states that this separation and recognized difference is the result of a divine work of grace upon the believer.

The father of the writer owned a Southern plantation. He had a brand for his cotton bales and a mark for his hogs, so there was no trouble in telling his property from those of his neighbors. We well remember his brand for the cattle. It consisted of two large iron letters F. C. attached to a frame and handle of like material. The iron brand was heated red hot and then applied suddenly to the hind quarters of a bullock or heifer. Through scorching hair and shriveling skin down went the burning letters into the flesh. The cattle would bellow, plunge, and run, but they were marked! The "F. C." was literally burned into them and stayed there. Change of weather never affected those letters. Years rolled by, but the mark remained. The hair never grew back again over the brand. So there was no trouble in telling my father's flocks from the other herds that were roaming around.

Has not God as distinctive a mark for His people? Can He not brand His followers in a way that everybody will see that they are the Lord's?

We thank God for the baptism of the Holy Ghost and Fire, for the flame and mark of sanctification which burns the letters J. C. (Jesus Christ) upon the Christian. It makes a marked crowd. It creates a peculiar people.

Something is done in sanctification that utterly spoils God's people for this world. They become out and out for God. They make no affinity with Ahab, do not go down to Egypt for horses, trust not in chariots, but in the living God whom they serve.

They desire no compromise with sin and the world, but "walk in God's statutes," "keep His judgments," pronounce the whole word shibboleth, stand up for the entire Gospel, are willing to be photographed in the dark, and are ready for heaven every moment of their lives.

Who is willing to be branded, and become God's peculiar people, seen and known of all men? May the Lord increase His own ten thousand times ten thousand, until sin and sinners shall be displaced everywhere, and the land redeemed for the possession, rulership and enjoyment of Christ and His saints.

CHAPTER XIII.

MOODS—AFFINITIES—AND IMPRESSIONS.

IT is blessed to be sanctified, and even more blessed to be intelligently sanctified. Happy is the man who enjoys the blessing of perfect love in connection with an informed mind, experienced head and sound judgment.

He who reads, thinks and compares has always an advantage over the thoughtless man or the mere creature of impulse. Especially is this seen in the sanctified life. Mr. Wesley says that great grace does not always mean great light, and so we see very excellent people being betrayed into grave mistakes and doing some very silly and reprehensible things.

If Satan can not keep the locomotive from leaving the depot, he tries to jump aboard and run it. If he can not keep us from taking in the heavenly fire, he endeavors to introduce false fire. In various ways he tries to derail, deflect, side-track and upset the purified whom God would bring through lives of great usefulness into heaven.

Then it is to be remembered we are at the bottom of a great atmospheric ocean, that we are bundles of nerves and sensibilities acted on by persons and things

In a most powerful and puzzling way, and so we need to study and know ourselves as well as the great grace of God within us. After getting the heart filled with the Holy Ghost it is well to get the head filled with the very facts and truth that should be there. The Bible speaks of grace and knowledge. They go well together.

We ought to understand the experience we possess, and comprehend in a measure the physical instrument on which it plays, or house in which it abides. There are curious cords and connections running up and down and through this complex mental and physical dwelling like so many bell wires. Sometimes God rings them, sometimes Satan touches the cord, and sometimes it may be only the weather affecting us. It is well to understand the different touches; it would save many a mistake and many a heartache. Hence that person is well advanced in spiritual wisdom who can distinguish here.

MOODS.

Among these fleeting, puzzling feelings are Moods. To the recently regenerated and sanctified nothing is so startling and terrifying at times. They are ready to give up hope and surrender their confidence without a reason save that they feel that certain puzzling and contradictory frames of mind and conditions of heart have taken possession of them, and they think therefore, that they can not be all right.

It is hard at times to account for moods. Bright ones may come from an exhilarating breeze and good digestion, while dark spells may spring from causes far removed from moral agencies, and where the soul has been and still is perfectly loyal to God.

An overflow of animal spirits is not to be regarded as levity and so repented of. It is simply to be watched and quietly controlled and guided as it can be. In the regenerated life the overflow is often allowed to go almost into a hysterical condition, when loud laugh is added to laugh, anecdote follows anecdote of mirthful character until spiritual harm is wrought.

But it is easy for the sanctified to control this freshet, and distribute what is really good in itself all over the Christian life in even, smooth, irrigating channels, and so turn what might have been a disaster into a benediction.

Sad moods are more puzzling to the sanctified. Having been told of the everlasting joy of the purified they marvel at the pensiveness which steals over them at times and sinks them into meditative silence.

Again we say there need be no sin in this. Some melancholy does spring from having done wrong, but not every pensive spirit that comes over the sanctified heart originates from transgression. On the contrary, the feeling we speak of is known to arise when the individual is living close to God and in perfect obedience to His will.

Pensiveness may spring from a high and holy state. It must be remembered that this world is not the home of the soul. The conditions and environments about us are not what are to be when the spirit is at its best in the unveiled presence of God. Some days as it flutters with indescribable longings and a consciousness of unfolded powers against the physical limitations, the body feels like a cage to it. The soul was made to soar, and here it is shut in by narrow walls of clay. It was made for abodes of love, purity and heavenly glory, and here it is projected in the midst of squalor, ugliness, violence and sin. Then it longs to see God. When shall I see my Father's face and in His bosom rest? All this and more will suddenly surge upward in the heart, and the person will be noticed with fixed, far-away gaze, and mute lips, absorbed in melancholy reverie. A very little thing may have brought it about—the stroke of a bell, the smell of a wild flower, the coo of a dove, some one singing a hymn in the distance, or the sight of a gold and crimson sunset. At once the mighty longing arose to be away from a world of pain, strife, oppression, wrong and sin, and to be with Christ where the body will never sicken, the mind never be shocked, or the heart wrung again. So was it that David said: "Oh, that I had wings like a dove for then would I fly away and be at rest!" So was it Paul said, "I long to depart." And so the Saviour Himself seemed to have a homesick feeling sweep for a moment over him in the seventeenth chapter of John when He speaks to His Father about the glory He had with Him before the world was. There is no sin necessarily in this temporary pensive tinge of the mind. It is only a proof of another and better life, of a happier world, and of the fact that we have not yet entered upon it. The soul is not hurt by such feelings, and they only become sinful and injurious when we indulge them to such an extent as to lapse into moping, repining, and neglect of duty.

Somehow the soul is richer for these very moments, provided we use them right and they keep us not from Christian work. They should bind us all the more to the life and world to come. The battle is still on, and it is not yet time to lay aside the armor. Paul longed to depart and be with Christ, but full of a healthy Christian life he said: "Nevertheless, to abide in the flesh is more needful for you." And so he remained, warning, rebuking, comforting and saving people, and like his Lord, going everywhere and doing good.

AFFINITIES.

Here is something we approach with considerable hesitation. Its very gravity makes us feel that a stronger pen should deal with the subject, and there is a natural fear of saying either too much or too little on the subject. Perhaps it is best to be brief.

We have all observed that while there is a spirit of

love and feeling of general good will among God's people, yet there are peculiar friendships and affections cherished for a few individuals as distinguished from the multitude. These special attachments seemed to be based upon, or originate from, consanguinity of temperament, similarity of taste and education, sameness of work, and other correspondences.

Thus far in the case we are still in the realms of innocence and see simply the working of natural laws in pure lives. All of us feel these natural preferences. From these come our best friends. Our Saviour Himself had a closer relation to Peter, John and James, and a special fondness for the home at Bethany.

A Christian writer once said he loved everybody, but liked a few. He meant by the word "like" that feeling which springs from agreeable fellowship and perfect understanding. All of us know what it is to love people in a religious way, whose notions, prejudices, habits and conduct make them distasteful and offensive to us. We love them, but do not care to make companions out of them. While there are others no better spiritually, but who possess the smile, manner, spirit, tastes, opinions and life we admire, and at once we realize the peculiar friendship or affection.

Thus far, we repeat, there is no wrong or harm done. The word of warning is that harm may come. Satan is especially wide awake and active at such times and places to make harm.

MOODS—AFFINITIES—IMPRESSIONS. 173

Many lovely Christians have gone unscathed through life along this very path. Earth has been made brighter, and heaven will be richer for the experience. But some have allowed the Adversary to trip them, and have fallen by the way, suddenly slain like Amasa, while multitudes passing by looked in amazement and grief upon the prostrate form that first wallowed, then became still, and then was covered up by command. After that, says the Bible, the people passed on.

When these "affinities" between the sexes begin to make one or the other or both to fret and repine over their present providential lot; when the kindred spirit feeling leads to private and public remarks reflecting on one joined to the speaker by laws of God and man; when the affair begets an epistolary correspondence between the parties that is more frequent than home letters; then peril is near, and sin is in full sight.

It would be very easy to give some ghastly facts here, but we, after considerable reflection, feel that it is best to leave the subject without further development.

Suffice it to say that the instincts of a pure heart, the general good sense of the world as crystalized in public opinion, and the blessed touches and whispers of the Holy Spirit will be all-sufficient to guide and teach us in this matter as in all others. It should not be forgotten, however, that the same Book which forbids evil also says, "Abstain from all *appearance* of evil." It is not only that evil and the appearance of evil are not long separated, but the Lord does not want the slightest indication of sin in the life of His child.

IMPRESSIONS.

Again we approach a most important topic. Like other things in the spiritual life, it has a true as well as a false side.

There are impressions that come directly from God. The Bible teaches this fact, and we are to look for them, and obey them when they come. Every spiritual person knows what it is to be led by the Spirit. Glances, touches, gentle movements and impulses from Him have been sufficient to stop us or lead forward, as the case may be, and we knew beyond all question that it was God's own hand on us, His voice within us, His Spirit impelling or restraining us that was leading us into all truth. How sweet it is to speak or be silent, to do or not to do as He inwardly bids us! Very close is such a walk, and very blessed is such a life thus abandoned to the Holy Ghost.

But there are "impressions" not of God. They may come with heavenly garb and religious manner and even using the Word of God. Some of these are born in our own hearts, are nurtured by our own fancies, and are shaped by our own preferences. Others come directly from the infernal world. John warns us against them. He tells us we are to "try the spirits, whether they be of God."

So here is the distinct assertion in the Word, that different spirits come to the soul, not only the Spirit of God, but evil spirits from beneath. If possible, says the apostle, they would "deceive the very elect." And there is no question but they have deceived some of the elect.

The idea is, do not suppose every impression is from God even though it come in the name of religion. Do not think every fancy is God's command; and that every rigid idea and extreme notion is God's desire. Many have so thought, and great has been the confusion in Israel, the trouble to the individual Christian, and the joy in hell.

People have forgotten that Satan was once an angel in heaven, that he has seen and been with God, has heard Him talk, and can talk like Him. It is wonderful how He can quote Scripture, how he helps people to consecrate, and how willingly he would take charge of the Christian life and run it in a way that will ultimately side-track or ditch the train.

We had best not be in too great a hurry with impressions. The Bible itself teaches us to be careful and take time, in the words, "He that believeth shall not make haste." The man of true faith will inquire of God before taking steps that are full of gravity and importance. Moses and Gideon did not spring to the front with the first impression that came to them; they waited for others, found they were of God and then went forward irresistibly and triumphantly.

Some will not do this, but follow every will-of-the-wisp hallucination of the mind, and every Jack-o' lantern religious teacher that comes around.

All of us know people who are ready for the latest craze in spiritual things. Like the Athenians they are open for every new thing. A strange doctrine, a curious physical manifestation, a piece of unneeded martyrology, sudden ascetic notions, fanciful interpretations of Scripture, unnatural conduct at home, a desire to lash everybody not thinking or doing as they do—all these and many more such things become predominant with them, are duly received and acted out, and with much assurance attributed to God.

One expression, "God told me" or "God impressed me" is familiar to us all. In one of our Western States we heard the sacred, solemn sentence uttered so frequently, lightly, unadvisedly, and at times so untruly that the heart ached and the soul fairly sickened.

God told one that he could eat breakfast. Though why the Lord should speak thus, when nature was clamoring through hunger for the same breakfast, opened a great field of doubt in the hearer's mind. God does not have to tell people to eat, drink and sleep, when he has arranged natural voices in the body that speak so clearly and unmistakably and know so well how to have their wishes attended to.

Another one left his church. "God told him," he said. Afterward, he came back, applied for membership and was restored. According to this man the Lord had made a mistake.

A lady known to the writer prepared three bowls of hot soup for three tired Christian workers. Just as they sat down, had said grace, and were about to partake of the warming and palatable repast, this lady was suddenly "impressed" to lead in prayer. Down they all went on their knees, and as the sister had great liberty that afternoon she prayed nearly twenty minutes. When they arose the soup was cold, stiff and unpalatable. Some with ascetic ideas, and Dark Age notions of penance might say God was in the matter; but the writer for one does not so believe. He has an idea that He who prepared a warm meal of bread and fish on the coals by Lake Galilee for His disciples and called them to it, did not object to His three tired followers having warm soup on that cold afternoon of which we speak, and so did not send the "impression" the sister labored under.

In one of the meetings conducted by the author, a lady greatly given to "impressions" came to him and with a most mysterious air whispered that "God had revealed to her that a certain young Christian worker on the ground was possessed with the devil." In less than an hour afterwards this very young man came to the writer and said that "God had shown or revealed to him that this very old lady was possessed with a number of devils." Comment is unnecessary.

In New England we saw a man who was placarded all over with Scripture texts, and religious phrases. The word "Time" was written on one leg, the word "Eternity" on the other. "Sin," as I recall, was on one arm, "Salvation" on the other. The word "Repent" was on his back, while lower down the coat was "Jesus is coming."

He said "God impressed him." Many of us did not believe a word of it. And as we studied the effect on the crowd, we saw not a single person solemnized, but people were either lamenting the mistaken act or smiling or laughing outright at the spectacle. A few days afterward we beheld him on a crowded street in a large city. The effect produced on all whom I could see, by this belittling and degradation of divine things, was most unhappy. Paul speaks of epistles written in flesh and blood by the finger of God; but this man made an epistle out of his clothes with a paint brush. We never heard of any one being "cut to the heart" and "crying out for mercy" to God on beholding this strange self-commissioned Gospel advertiser.

We have received letters asking for certain large sums of money. They said "God told them" to write and ask us. All this sounded strangely, when the Lord knew at the time we did not have over a couple of dollars and had no means of raising more. Other letters have come in the way of rebuke telling us "God impressed them to do so." In them we have been told to do what we were already doing, and not to do what we were not doing.

A man in one of our Central Western States had been a most powerful and useful minister of the Gospel. By and by he began to have "impressions." One was that marriage was an impure relation. It was vain that the "Word" said, "Marriage is honorable among ALL and the bed undefiled"; the "impression" was bigger than the Bible with him. After awhile he put away his wife, and then left his children. He had an "impression" that all natural affections were wrong. So in obedience to "impressions" he forsook the wife that God told him to cleave to, and allowed his forsaken children to struggle for themselves, when the Book says that a man who does not provide for his household is worse than an infidel.

We have known people under "impressions" to seek for new and strange experiences, when that apostolic man, John Wesley, says: "If we seek for anything but more love we are certain to land in error." Alas for it, we have witnessed such landings.

We have seen people under the plea "God told

me" become intolerant, fault-finding intermeddlers and busy-bodies. In striking at the "pride of life" they developed that most horrible of all forms, spiritual pride, and did not know it. In a plea for zeal, they presented us a Jehu cutting and slashing, instead of a Jesus healing and binding up.

We feel that we could not do a better thing than attach a quotation from Mr. Wesley, in regard to these very things :

1. "Watch and pray continually against pride. If God has cast it out, see that it enter no more; it is fully as dangerous as evil desire, and you may slide back into it unawares, especially if you think there is no danger of it. 'Nay, but I ascribe all I have to God.' So you may and be proud nevertheless; for it is pride not only to ascribe anything we have to ourselves, but to think we have what we really have not. You ascribe all the knowledge you have to God, and in this you are humble. But if you think you have more than you really have, or if you think you are so taught of God as to no longer need man's teaching, pride lieth at the door. Do not, therefore, say to any that would advise or reprove you : 'You are blind ; you can not teach me.' Always remember, much grace does not imply much light. These do not always go together. To imagine none can teach you but those who are themselves saved from sin is a very great and dangerous mistake. Give not place to it for a moment. It will lead you into a thousand other mistakes and that irrevocably. Obey and regard them that are over you in the Lord, and do not think you know better than

they; know their plan and your own: always remembering, 'Much love does not imply much light.'

2. "Beware of that daughter of pride, 'enthusiasm' [meaning fanaticism]. Keep at the utmost distance from it; give no place to a heated imagination. Do not hastily ascribe things to God. Do not easily suppose dreams, voices, impressions, visions, and revelations to be from God. They may be from him, they may be from nature, they may be from the devil. Therefore believe not every spirit, but try the spirits whether they be of God. Try all things by the written Word, and let all bow down before it. You are in danger of enthusiasm every hour if you depart ever so little from Scripture; yea, from the plain literal meaning of any text taken in connection with the context."

We can now see why John said, "Try the spirits whether they be of God." He adds that many false prophets have gone out into the world. And Paul writes that "In the latter times some shall depart from the faith, giving heed to seducing spirits and doctrines of devils—forbidding to marry and commanding to abstain from meats which God hath created to be received with thanksgiving of them which believe and know the truth."

We are to try the spirits, and always with the Word of God. There must be a "Thus saith the Lord" for every whisper of the Spirit. God does not act contradictorily. He will not say with His Word one thing and with His Spirit another. So let us bring every impression to the Bible, and there examine it. If God's Book tells us to love and cherish our families let us do it. If Christ prepares us for hard treatment on account of the Truth then do not let us become frightened and run at the first sign of being martyred. The impression may say, "Fly," but the Word says, "Leap for joy and rejoice when ye are persecuted for righteousness' sake." If when we are misunderstood, treated coldly, unjustly and cruelly, and the impression is strong to return railing for railing, criticism for criticism, and abuse for abuse; before we do it let us bring the impression to the Word and hear what God says. If the Book reads that we are to draw the sword, and give as hard cuts and blows as we receive in wrong treatment, then let us do so. But what does it say? "Put up thy sword, for they that live by the sword shall perish by the sword," and again, "If when ye do well and suffer for it ye take it patiently, this is acceptable with God."

Let us try the "impressions," whether they agree with the Word. If they can stand that test, if they breathe the spirit of Christ, we can stand by them and for them. If the Word is against them, then the sooner we cast them away, the better it will be for mind, body and soul, for family, friends and church, and for our present happiness and usefulness, as well as salvation to come.

CHAPTER XIV.

DOUBTS—FEARS—AND FRET

EVERY form of life has its peculiar enemies. We have only to look around us on the animal world, notice the flight of birds, and watch the swift rush and sparkling leaps of fish from the water, to see that on land or sea or in the air every kind of life is in danger, and much of the time is spent in flying from enemies.

The intellectual life has its peril; and diet, medicine and travel are resorted to for its protection.

The spiritual life has likewise its adversaries, and so the Bible abounds in warnings and directions. The sanctified life, with all its superior grace and power, is not exempt from danger. Not simply does Satan make violent assaults upon such a character, and not only does the sanctified man find a peculiarly bitter human opposition on his announcement of the possession of the grace, but there are formidable foes along mental and spiritual lines. Inbred sin is indeed cast out and the heart is pure, but the man is still a free moral agent and can lose the heavenly light and fall, as did Adam in the Garden of Eden.

One class of these internal foes are,—

DOUBTS.

It is wonderful how Satan tries to insinuate the spirit of doubt again into the soul that has been so blessed and filled by a perfect trust in God and His Word. He knows that we obtained the great blessing by Faith, and so his great battles, his frequent subtle attacks are made just at that point. Let the sanctified recall the past and see how often he has felt this peculiar attack made upon his faith.

The adversary is well aware that if he can get the soul to doubting the door of the life is then open for him to come in and do as he will.

Faith is the condition of salvation, the measure of salvation and the only means of retaining what we have. The Bible says "the just shall live by faith," and again "without faith it is impossible to please God."

Doubt is the direct opposite of faith. Faith believes every word of God; Doubt does not. Faith trusts the Divine Providence, while Doubt laments and gives up at every dark shadow. Faith obeys God; Doubt disobeys.

The history of the Fall in Paradise can be traced back to Doubt. God had said that if Adam and Eve ate of the forbidden tree they should die. Satan said they would not die. The man and his wife *believed* Satan and *doubted* God. With the cherished doubt of course came the sinful act soon after, and they fell. The crash of that fall has never ceased to echo and re-echo in this and other worlds. They found that day when driven out from the divine presence that to doubt God is a fearful thing.

The dreadful ruin of King Saul began with his doubting the word of the Lord. God had told him to slay a certain Canaanitish nation, men, women, children, animals and all. It was a wise, and scholars will tell you that it was a merciful command as well. But Saul saw fit not to obey. He obeyed partially, sparing many of the best looking animals. When Samuel met him and asked if he had done what God had commanded, he replied that he had. Samuel's rejoinder was: "What meaneth then this bleating of sheep and lowing of oxen that I hear?" The king's reply was that he had spared the best of the cattle for sacrifice. Samuel's solemn answer was: "To obey is better than sacrifice." Then followed the words that God had rejected him for his disobedience. From that day the man fell rapidly, until at last, a few years afterward, he takes his own life on Mt. Gilboa. The ruin began by doubting the word of God; the doubt leading to disobedience, and the disobedience to his ruin.

Perhaps nothing could more deeply wound the reader of these lines than for a person to doubt his word. Men knock each other down for such things.

To be called a liar is a deep insult. To be said that one is unreliable is simply to say they can not be trusted, their word can not be taken, that they are without character.

Why is it that as people see these things they do not remember them when applied to God. God has a Word, God has made promises and threats. He says good will come to us if we do right, and trouble, sorrow, shame and pain if we do wrong. Whoever goes into sin after that simply doubts God. Whoever gets discouraged in time of evil opposition doubts God, for He said He would deliver us. Whoever gives up his religious life and experience because of fears of the present and future doubts God, for He said He would keep us to the end, and no one should pluck us from His hand. In a word, to listen to Satan, sin, temptations, evil people, and give heed to a sinking, drooping heart, is to doubt God. And to doubt God is a most grave and calamitous thing.

Look at it in any light, and we see that faith is the condition of salvation, that we live by it, that we conquer by it, that we please God through it, and that Doubt is a heinous thing to allow to enter the mind and dwell in the heart.

We marvel that we hear apologies for doubt; that people should get up in public and say "they have so many doubts," and sit down as if they had not said one of the ghastliest things in the moral vocabulary.

God has spoken, but they doubt. God has said certain things, but they doubt. God has promised to bring His children through every trial and sorrow, but they are filled with doubts!

It is said that Mr. Spurgeon came one evening to a meeting of his elders, and rubbing his hands before the fire said: "Brethren, I have just gotten the victory over some fearful doubts." To his surprise no answer was made. So he repeated the sentence, and as they were still silent asked them why they said nothing. The reply of one of his officers was remarkable. He said:

"Why did you not say as you came in that you just had a great victory over an inclination to steal a horse? For which is worse, to steal a horse or to admit that you doubt God and His Word?"

Mr. Spurgeon said he never forgot the power of that rebuke, for he felt it was true. So may our readers be profited by the incident.

We all have friends and relatives whom no tongue nor circumstance could make us doubt. Is not God truer, better, more faithful in an infinite degree than they? How, then, can we doubt Him?

So let it be understood at once among us as sanctified people, that because faith is the condition of spiritual life and safety, because it is the victory that overcometh the world, because by it we please God, and because we can not afford to doubt such a Being as our Lord, therefore we will not allow doubts of Him, of His word to us, His work in us, and His promises for the present and future, ever to enter our minds and hearts, with their sickening, saddening, paralyzing influence again.

Do not stop to ask how one is to keep doubts out. To sanctified people it should be the easiest of things.

How do people keep snakes out of the hall or gallery? They sweep them out into the yard with the broom as fast as they would crawl in. So when doubts wriggle and squirm towards you, take the broom of a resolute will and sweep them out. Say, I will not let them in. And if you say that, they can not come in. This is exercising faith. Refusing to doubt is believing. How simple and blessed!

FEARS.

Here is a class of mental states that bear a strong family resemblance to doubts. In point of time they follow doubts, or are originated by them. There is certainly some connection between them, for they are always found together.

To be full of faith is to be full of courage, and to doubt is to fear.

In speaking of fears we are not stating that they fill and dominate the sanctified life. On the contrary, sanctification if it does anything delivers from fear. The Word of God settles this when it declares that

"Perfect love casteth out all fear," and again, "Ye have received not the spirit of bondage again to fear." While the view of the disciples after they received the Baptism of the Holy Ghost shows them completely delivered from fear. Men raged while they rejoiced. The Sanhedrim had them scourged, but they preached on. The powers of the church threatened them with death if they persisted in their Gospel ministry, and the reply of the disciples was, "Now, Lord, behold their threatenings," and went on preaching just the same. The truly sanctified soul ought to be fearless. According to the Scripture this is the true state of the man in the enjoyment of the blessing.

Yet we are free moral agents still, and sensibilities are left, and Satan is not dead, and in many ways he tries to project into the heart that which has been burned out by the Holy Ghost. He points to lions in the way, to the ridicule of people, the opposition of persons high in authority, and all the numerous adverse influences that surround us. Oh, how he would like to get the sanctified soul looking at these things long enough to allow forgotten tremors to revisit the heart! How he loves to scare God's people, and keep them scared! To send them forth with a timid, brow-beaten, handshaking, cowering, ready-to-run kind of air! How he would love to introduce them in this pitiable condition to earth and hell as God's soldiers with which He is to conquer the world.

The truly sanctified man will not be caught in this way. But in spite of Satanic bluster will go forward, and lo, under the whisper and light of Christ he will see that the lions are chained, that the ridicule can be borne, that the opposition will be buried, and that as for adverse influences they are far outnumbered by mightier heavenly forces, for "they that be with us are more than they that be with them."

In the tenth chapter of Matthew the Saviour singles out some of the things that are most dreaded by men, and attaches a "Fear not" to each one of them. Let the reader glance at them:

Rejected in towns and homes;

Delivered up to Councils;

Scourged in synagogues;

Forsaken by one's own family;

Hated of all men;

Called a devil; and

The household become a foe.

About them all Christ says, "Fear not."

The disciples were faithful pupils, and under the Baptism of Fire and these strong reassuring words of Christ they did not fear. May we, with the like Baptism and the same Saviour by us, around us and in us, be also undismayed and go on from faith to faith and victory to victory, until at last we hear the "Well done" and enter into the joy of our Lord.

We were much struck once with a speech that fell

from the lips of a world-famous colored female evangelist. She said that sanctified as she was, and had been for twenty-five years, Satan now and then tried to trip her from her steadfastness in Christ by bringing up memories of the awful past; but that she knew how to meet him. Then suddenly straightening herself up she said:

"If I was in a splendid chariot driving up one of the broad avenues of one of our greatest cities, and driven by the Archangel Gabriel, and the Devil stood on the sidewalk looking on and mocking, and should cry out, 'Look at Amanda Smith sitting up there. I knew her when she was a poor colored washerwoman, and I know all the mean things she once said and did' —what would I do? Would I get out of the carriage and take to side streets and alleys to hide because of what Satan said? No, sir! I would not even look around, but I would raise my head and say, 'Drive on, Gabriel'."

Who of us have not suffered in this way from recollections of a sinful past? If dwelt upon they terrorize the heart and paralyze the life. May we all imitate this woman of faith, and forgetting the past because God says He does, and remembering what Christ has done for us and in us, may we look straight ahead and cry out in answer to every voice that would stop us, "Drive on!"

FRET.

When we become sanctified the spirit of fret is taken out of us. Originating in Inbred Sin, when that is burned out by the Baptism of Fire we cease of course to worry.

One of the loveliest features of sanctification is that when we have the genuine blessing we do not fret and have no inclination to do so. Outside circumstances and conditions have not changed, but we are changed. The inward spiritual fever, the gunpowdery element, the easily aroused irritability and its concomitant spirit of worry are all gone.

It is all very easy for a preacher to take the text, "Fret not thyself in anywise to do evil," and urge this upon regenerated people. As long as Inbred Sin is in the soul Christians will fret. And so the congregation which heard the sermon on not worrying, and praised it to the preacher's face, went home and worried. And the preacher who delivered the discourse went home and fretted; his wife, children and servants being witnesses.

Sanctification takes the spirit of fret out of the heart. But we must remember that the causes of irritation remain in the world, no matter how gloriously we were sanctified. It is the work of Satan to get the attention of sanctified people once more on these objects of worry or causes for fret. The next effort is to secure a few remarks on the subject in the way of honest criticism and what he calls godly judgment. Then follow some more remarks, as they easily will after the levee of a God-established silence is broken. Before the man knows it Satan has crept in through the critical eye and judging mouth, and sowed the seeds of worry and fret again.

We have all heard of "Sour Godliness." Of all forms of religious life, yes, of any kind of life, it is the most repelling. Such people have not lost the light, but the sweetness of the Gospel; the knowledge is left, but the grace of the Lord Jesus is gone. Knowing God and the Saviour as the world knows them not, yet they have allowed Satan to resow Inbred Sin; the manna has corrupted, the honey of Canaan has been turned to vinegar and gall, the spirit of fret has returned, the sour-godly man is abroad.

We reaffirm that sanctification takes worry out of the soul, but the causes for fret still remain. There are so many things that are not done as they should be. You see personal peculiarities about Holiness people, and objectionable mannerisms in Holiness preachers that are distressing. You observe a lack of education and culture among people who make claims to high religious experiences. Certain methods adopted in revival work do not seem to be wise or best or Scriptural. You notice startling inconsistencies and even appearances of evil among those claiming to be sanctified. You hear of lapses, backslidings and dreadful falls. You mark the coldness and supineness of the laity, the timidity and man-fear of the preachers, and in a word a score of things that try the faith and patience and tempt you to give up at length in despair.

The Ark is coming up, but it is drawn by cows on an ox-cart. The slowest of animals pulling, and the ungainliest of vehicles drawing the beautiful holy Ark of God. Surely this is all wrong. The Ark should have been placed on a golden chariot and drawn by milk-white horses! Surely something is wrong when rich, great, and prominent people have nothing to do with the beautiful blessing of Heart Purity and Perfect Love. Why is it that so many poor, obscure, illiterate and uncultured people are harnessed to the great Holiness movement of to-day? What rough-looking messengers, what uncouth manners, what unimposing tabernacles, sheds and places of worship! Then how slow the movement toward Jerusalem and the Temple, where the Ark ought to be! It looks like it would never get there. Here and there an Obed-Edom opens his heart and home for the Ark, but most of the time it is on the road, a spectacle and gazing-stock to the Philistines. Then the oxen stumble, and David gets discouraged, and Michal is laughing at the window—behold, everybody seems to be against us.

Now what a time to fret! What an opportunity for calling of conventions of protest, and filling the papers with letters of bitter arraignment of men and the times, with side dishes of remarks acidulated and made hot with ecclesiastical vinegar and pepper.

What a time for discouragement, and toning down the testimony, and becoming politic, and dropping certain objectionable Bible terms, and as you foresee squally times ahead, making friends with those whom you would have receive you into their habitations. Now is the opportunity to write long epistles to religious journals bemoaning the Holiness movement, and rapping and slapping at the people who believe in it. Verily, if a man will write such a letter, or put forth a pamphlet after this order, all the sins which he has sinned in formerly believing in and professing the experience shall be forgiven him—in this world.

There is no end to causes for fret as we glance over the work and field. Shall we do it? Or shall we hear God and follow the blessed command, "Fret not thyself in any wise to do evil"? It is bound to result in evil if we do. As sanctification took out the worrying spirit, let it in God's name stay out.

And let this thought be for our comfort, that God is in the Holiness movement, and He is well able to take care of it. He preserved the truth and the Church centuries before we were born, and He will do so centuries after we have gone to dust. He buried the generation that tried to keep His people out of Canaan, and He will do so again to-day. He swept aside Herod, and Pilate, and Julian the Apostate, and Nero, and all of His people's enemies, in spite of their bluster, cruelty, pomp and power, and they are to-day under the ground waiting for the Judgment Day. In like manner He will overthrow sooner or later every denier and resister of His holy truth, and every oppressor and persecuter of His holy people, and either smitten like Uzzah on earth for touching the Ark, or judged at the last day for oppressing the Lord's servants, they will surely have their reward. A great unrelenting justice will settle that matter, in spite of protesting cries of "Lord, Lord, in thy name we did many wonderful works." A cry swept away forever by words as solemn as doom, "Inasmuch as ye did it to them, ye did it to me," and again, "I know ye not."

There is no need to fret. God is alive and working. And the Ark is coming up the road in spite of surrounding ignorant Philistines, in spite of the feeble social and ecclesiastical agencies that God is using to bring it up, and in spite of the distance still between us and Jerusalem. The Ark will finally get there. David and Jerusalem will come out to meet it, and with great rejoicings the long-banished Ark, the long-lost doctrine of Holiness by Faith will be restored to its place in the Temple and churches of God.

When it is done, no flesh will be able to glory. It was not man that did it. Man could not do it. God did it in spite of man, in spite of the authority and power of Church and State. God did not do it with the great, rich, prominent, eloquent and elegant; if He had, the world would have believed that the work was accomplished by human greatness, wealth, position, eloquence and culture, and God would have lost the glory. Oh, the wisdom of God and the power of God; He brought the Ark up to Jerusalem, not on a beautiful vehicle drawn by handsome animals with tossing manes and glittering harness, but on an ox-cart drawn by lowing cows. "For ye see your calling, brethren, how that not many wise men after the flesh, not many mighty, not many noble are called: but God hath chosen the foolish things of this world to confound the wise; and God hath chosen the weak things of the world to confound the things which are mighty, and base things of the world, and things which are despised hath God chosen, yea and things which are not, to bring to naught things that are; that no flesh should glory in his presence."

Mr. Wesley said he would as soon expect to swear as to fret. And why not? For fretting is the very essence of unbelief, and the Bible tells us that unbelief will damn us.

We have a preacher friend in the North. One day he was in a carriage being driven rapidly to the depot to catch a train. He had but a few minutes to reach the station and purchase the ticket before the express would be due. It was very important that he should leave on that particular train. Just as he had come in a short distance of the depot, a great lumbering freight train pulled in before him, the street gates were shut down and he had to wait for one of the longest trains he ever saw go bumping by in a snail-gait way. What a time for fret, what a golden opportunity for worry, fuming and general inward perspiration. He could have held his watch in his hand, and said: "Will the train never end? I will never get to the depot in time," and boiled over generally. This is what many would have done, and gained nothing in the world by such fretting except the evil the Bible speaks of.

Our friend was a sanctified man. So when the long train blocked his way, he leaned back quietly and as one box thumped by he said, "Glory." A second car passed and he cried "Hallelujah," a third was honored with the words "Bless the Lord," and toward the fourth box was propelled the glad and exultant old word of "Glory" again. But by the time he had uttered these expressions of praise the fourth time, he was shouting happy, and the carriage could hardly contain him. He got such a blessing that he did not care whether he was left or not. He obtained one of the greatest blessings of his life by saying "Hallelujah" over an obstructing train and crying out "Glory" over every box-car that crossed the track before him. In a word, he refused to fret. A charming sequel to the incident was that God delayed the express train for his servant ten minutes, so that our brother had time to purchase his ticket and get off without hurry. To sum up, by obeying God he not only got off on the train he desired, but secured also a wonderfully rich blessing in addition, with which to travel and rejoice all the evening.

May we do likewise? May we not count the great obstructions that we see piling up to stop our way, but praise God over those that bump and clatter by us. We will have nothing to do with the language of fret that belongs to the carnal mind, but speak in the heavenly vernacular of adoration and praise. Instead of wailing over mistakes and failures we will shout over our deliverances. Instead of nursing our sorrows and wrongs we will sing praises to God, if we have to do it at midnight with feet in stocks and backs riven by the scourge. In a word, we will take Habakkuk, out of whom all the spirit of fret seems to have gone, as an example, when he says: "Although the fig tree shall not blossom, neither shall fruit be in the vines; the labour of the olive shall fail, and the fields shall yield no meat; the flock shall be cut off from the fold, and there shall be no herd in the stalls: yet will I rejoice in the Lord, I will joy in the God of my salvation."

CHAPTER XV.

COME-OUT-ISM AND PUT-OUT-ISM.

IN view of the suspicion, as well as unfriendliness, with which the blessing of entire sanctification and its possessors and professors are regarded in many quarters to-day, the question has been naturally raised, and that repeatedly, What shall we do?

Preachers are discounted who enjoy, preach and press this great blessing. Laymen who have it soon find they are regarded with suspicion and uneasiness, are removed from official positions, and in other cases even put out of the church. As for meetings held in church, hall, tent or brush arbor, they are looked upon with great disfavor by many in the church, are felt to be disloyal and hurtful to denominational interests, and are avoided, discountenanced, ridiculed and opposed, as the case may be

The profession of the experience in class-meeting, preachers' meeting and conference love feast, is received with chilling silence and drooping heads.

The subscribing to a religious paper published distinctively on this line is felt to be wrong, and is spoken against and legislated against in conferences.

A holiness literature is felt to be unneeded, and

holiness gatherings of all kinds to be deprecated and condemned.

This state of things and much more of the same sort exists and so extorts the question, What under the circumstances shall be done?

Numbers of questions and letters have been addressed to the author asking advice for individuals and for whole communities as well. The statement made by them was that the spirit of the century was against religious intolerance, that freedom of conscience was guaranteed by the constitution of this country, that the doctrine they contended for was imbedded in the writings and teachings of their church, and yet for defending it they were treated as schismatics. That if one year they had a pastor who believed in it, the next year another preacher was sent who opposed the doctrine, ridiculed the experience, and either adroitly or forcibly undid the work of years, done by holiness people on full salvation lines.

The question propounded was what should they do under the circumstances. Should they remain to be marked, tabooed, ostracized, and hear assailed from the pulpit Sabbath after Sabbath the experience which they enjoyed and the doctrine they knew to be divine? Or should they go to other denominations that are more friendly and tolerant? Or should they organize themselves into independent congregations?

After a great holiness revival, when fifty, one hundred or two hundred souls have swept into the blessing of Perfect Love the question arises again with increasing gravity. The thought of the people being left in the midst of a doubting and jeering community without a ministerial head and shepherd to feed and keep them together, and the additional fact of their peculiar danger of falling into the hands of false teachers who would switch them off into error and fanaticism; these facts are bound to spring the question, What shall be done under such a state of things?

And yet in the face of all this, when the question has been asked the writer, his pen has been used and his voice lifted against what is known as

COME-OUT-ISM.

Let it be understood at once that by come-out-ism we do not mean a change of church relationship. There are many good reasons that can arise in the lives of Christians to warrant and necessitate a transfer of membership from one denomination to the other. This has ever been practiced among the churches and has never that we heard of been called come-out-ism. There are many preachers in the Methodist Church who came there from other denominations. Some of them now occupy high positions, and no one regards them and calls them come-out-ers.

The come-out-ism that we refer to is a kind of ecclesiastical lawlessness, a spirit that will not brook control, despises authority, and is generally refractory. Such people quote the Scripture, "Come out of her, my people," as referring to religious denominations, and so sever all church relations, and rail upon what they call "Sects" and live ecclesiastically apart from their brethren.

Against this withdrawal and separation from the the church we have always lifted our voice. We grant that in many congregations we find spiritual deadness, formality and worldliness; we grieve over the amusement features, questionable financial methods and the presence of the cooking-stove and dining-room in the Church of God. We listen to a character of singing in some churches that we believe to be offensive to God. We hear oftentimes sermons that are rhetorical, literary and entertaining, but without spiritual food, and with no unction in them. And yet with all these things before us we have counseled the people to remain in the church, and for the following reasons:

First, if we have the wonderful experience we say we have, it is evidently intended of God as a light of the world and salt of the earth blessing for those who have it not.

If the church has lost it or never possessed the grace, we who have received so many benefits from the people of God, in simple gratitude alone owe it to them to stay with them and so teach and live the blessing that they also will obtain it.

The very figures of "light" and "salt" should reveal our duty. Salt is not to be removed to itself, but put on the meat it is to preserve. Light is sent to scatter darkness, not to draw off in a bunch to itself and leave it alone.

If our church friends do not see the second work of grace at once, we must remember that we also heard of it for years before we felt stirred up to seek and possess it. Our duty evidently is to stay by the ship in hopes that God will give us all the company who sail with us.

Second, to "come out," is finally to drift into some kind of organization, and the objection to that is seen in the following grave facts:

One is that we have enough of religious denominations already

Again, by coming out from the churches in which we were raised, we separate ourselves from the very body of people we want to teach and ought to bless. This movement is certain to raise an insurmountable wall in that direction. We have seen it in quite a number of places. Nor is this all, but we have seen this lofty and unscalable wall presented to Holiness workers and preachers who never dreamed of leaving the church. The doctrine was made to suffer from the mistakes of good people who acted hastily and unwisely. In such communities great bodies of excellent people will not hear the doctrine of sanctification preached, no matter who fills the pulpit, because their impression is that it rends and destroys instead of filling with the Holy Ghost and building up every interest of Zion.

Still again, the very things that have been deplored and inveighed against in the various churches will in due course of time be seen reproduced in any ecclesiastical organization. It may start out well, but certain regrettable things are sure in time to come in and break forth.

Some twelve or fifteen years ago a large body of Christians formed a Holiness Church in which there must be fully two hundred congregations. To-day they are rent over a question of church polity, the two wings standing one for Elder Supremacy and the other for Extreme Congregationalism. The opposite party dubbing the other side by one of the titles above.

We know of two preachers who said they were so domineered over and oppressed by church authorities that they drew out and left the fold. To-day they have a "following" and are ecclesiastical despots. I never saw a bishop or presiding elder more autocratic than are these same men.

In other quarters of our country there are leading laymen in the holiness movement who are on the high road to be popes. Yet they were once the humblest and most sweet-spirited of men.

With equal pain we have discovered in more than one holiness camp ground committee the same partialities, prejudices, man-fear, and secret way of doing things, that they as individuals had formerly condemned in Boards of Stewards.

These are sporadic cases, it is true, but are hints to us of what we are to expect if the holiness people "come out" and organize. God forbid that they should do so.

We are convinced that no greater calamity could befall the holiness movement than for it to separate from the church, and form into a distinct ecclesiastical organization. In a few years we would see the same things existing that we deplore to-day in certain religious quarters.

The third reason against "coming out" is that a witnessing of suffering on our parts to the truth of sanctification will be more convincing and effective in bringing people to the knowledge of the truth and into the experience itself than any other course.

The excuse given for Come-out-ism is that our traveling preachers are located; the licenses of local preachers are taken away, while our members are ridiculed and continually belabored from the pulpit in regard to the blessing they enjoy and which they know to be as true as heaven.

Ought we to remain, they ask, in such surroundings? and Sunday after Sunday, instead of hearing the gospel, be treated to this hour's tirade and abuse?

Our reply is that our sufferings are not worthy to

be compared with what the disciples and early Christians went through for the gospel's sake. Nor does it measure up to the mob violence inflicted upon early Methodists. Nor does it equal the harsh treatment given by the world to the Salvation Army before it became popular. Neither have we been martyred like the Apostles; nor treated like Mr. Wesley, who was stoned times without number; nor burned at the stake like the Reformers; nor butchered in cold blood for our faith like the Armenians.

We have been sent to broken-down appointments, located, and licenses taken away. We have been sat down on at Conference, attacked in our church papers, and ridiculed and called cranks and fanatics. We have been treated to any amount of "cold shoulder" and our stock value has gone down amazingly in our church councils. We have been laughed at publicly and privately, and been the butt and target of many tongues and pens—but we have not yet seen the prison or the stake, and God has said, "Touch not his life."

The question to my mind is, Can we not stand abuse? Can we not be laughed at, ridiculed and treated unjustly without straightway wanting to leave the church and withdraw support from the preachers! Can we not endure opposition? Will not the blessing of sanctification keep us sweet? Is not thy God, O Daniel, able to deliver thee from the lions?

God is to-day giving us the opportunity to prove

the blessing of sanctification to the church and world. The way He adopts for the illustration and vindication of the doctrine is by the course of ridicule, opposition and even persecution. "If when ye do well and suffer for it, ye take it patiently: this is acceptable with God." If when detracted, denounced and opposed we keep sweet, uncomplaining, loving and full of holy joy, we will convince gainsayers and doubters and bring about a sweeping holiness revival. It will take time, but we will win at last. It is the only way in which we can win the victory we crave to see.

If, on the other hand, we can not brook contradiction, but fly into controversies and disputes; if we will not wait for God to lock the lion's jaws or unlock the prison doors, and thus deliver us from our difficulties, but take things into our own hands and try to lock the lion's jaw ourself, and beat down the walls of our confinement with our own fists and weapons, then will the lion eat us up, or the prison wall fall on us.

If we, instead of keeping patient and waiting God's time, go to inveighing against laws and authorities, and abusing the church which baptized us, married us, buried our dead, taught us in our childhood and youth all we know of God, bore with us a thousand times; if we do this, who will believe we have perfect love, and who will want what we say we have?

If sanctification does not keep us patient, kind, long-suffering and forgiving, then in what respect does it differ from the ordinary type of religious living we see around us?

The soul as we have studied it need never be injured by hardship and oppression. Like violets, the spirit breathes out its sweetest perfume when downtrodden. Christ, the Bible tells us, was made perfect through suffering, and we read that if we suffer with Him we shall also reign with Him.

Let us stand firm and true, but be gentle and loving. Let us witness a good confession before the Pilates of this world. Let us rejoice like Peter when we are scourged, and go on preaching, testifying and living the experience. Let us pray for our stoners as did Stephen. Let us say with Paul no matter how we are treated that our prayer and desire for Israel is that it might be saved. Let us be "in the Spirit" even on Patmos, where we have been exiled to poor appointments for the truth, and write messages of thrilling power to the churches that will burn when we have gone to ashes. In a word, let us look up that overlooked passage in the fifth chapter of Matthew where the Saviour tells us to "love our enemies, bless them that curse you, do good to them that hate you, and pray for those which despitefully use and persecute you."

If anything in the world will convince our brethren that we have the second blessing, one ahead of them, it will be such a spirit and such a life.

Do not let us leave the church, but continue to come to the services, contribute to the collections, and always keep sweet. We should also have a regular holiness meeting at least once a week on some night that will not conflict with the regular church appointments. So, if we will do these things, if we will steadily follow this sweet, gentle and yet firm way we will move and win the people, disarm prejudice, remove resentment, and as David was asked to return to Jerusalem by the very people who drove him out, so shall we finally prevail and return to Zion with songs and everlasting joy.

PUT-OUT-ISM.

This we regard as very different from Come-outism. It is a treatment that has been visited upon the best people in the past ages, that has been repeated in these days, and will continue to be exercised, we fear, for years to come.

Divisions and parties seem to be as natural in State and Church as hemispheres are on this globe. Nothing makes a plainer line of distinction or digs a deeper channel of division than a marked grade in the religious life. Some have ever stood up for form, ceremony and church machinery and government, while others filled with the Spirit care little for those things save as God would have them regarded and duty and common sense see their actual fitness and need.

The Pharisees were great on the observances of the Law; the Sadducees were mighty in doctrinal discussion, and the Essenes went to the deserts and caves in lives of spiritual contemplation. The Catholic prelates in their glittering vestments, and Martin Luther pleading before them for the truth of justification by faith was a spectacle along the line we speak of. The clergy of the seventeenth century, engaged in the work professionally with relaxation of wine parties and fox hunts, while John Wesley and his followers preaching to the neglected masses and visiting the sick and prisoners and helping the poor, is another contrast.

The big religious conventions of to-day with famous speakers out-doing one another in the name of the Lord, and the holiness camp-meetings with altars crowded with weeping penitents and the fire falling from heaven, is another scene for the thoughtful. Also the stirring, fussy, unspiritual Ladies' Aid Society is in marked contrast to, and holds itself aloof from the class meeting room where testimonies ring clear, tears drip, and shouts abound.

We have men filling high positions in the church to-day who never save souls. Editors, college presidents, dignitaries and officials of various kinds; and yet preaching, writing, and moving around, they do not know what it is to see a conversion. On the other hand, we see another class of ministers, humble, obscure, poorly paid, many of them unlearned, but deeply religious and full of power, saving the souls of men wherever they go. Another curious fact is that the first mentioned class have the ruling influence in the church and manage everything, while the second class are ruled, and listen deferentially once or twice a year to big addresses and sermons from the first class. It is certainly a strange spectacle both to earth and heaven, to see a body of men who know how to save souls listening for an hour to instructions as to how to do it, when the instructor himself does not know how and never knew how.

These foregoing hints are given that the reader might see how divisions arise in the Church of God not only on questions of polity, but along the line of character and religious experience.

As a rule, the less spiritual part of the membership of the church is in the majority, and when this class handles the reins of power, hasty and oppressive measures are certain to come.

Naturally, the deeper spiritual experience and testimony of the minority will grieve and offend the majority, and so only too likely ridicule, criticism, opposition, and finally expulsion will be the fate of the smaller number.

This prepares one for Put-out-ism while still not believing in Come-out-ism. The last is a mistake, and is certain to end unhappily; the first is all right so far as the victim is concerned, who is sure to receive happiness and blessedness on earth and reward in heaven.

It is a sorrowful spectacle, however, to see people ridiculed, oppressed and sometimes ejected from the church on account of possessing a heart-warming, soul-overflowing religious experience. The Bible tells us about putting away the member who committed sin, but where will we find a Scripture that can cover and defend the course of thrusting people out of the ministry and church because they have received the Baptism of the Holy Ghost and are sanctified?

In some places where this has been done the reply is that it was not on account of the man's belief in a doctrine or profession of experience that he was turned out, but for general crankiness, insubordination and other faults. Laymen are said to refuse to bow to authority, and preachers are reported at Conference as unacceptable, and that work can not be found for them. By this method men filled with the Spirit of God and who have revivals every year have been cast out. Concerning the excuse given we only say that "The Great Day" will prove whether the charge was true or not. All hidden things shall be revealed in that hour.

In other places, and among denominations other than the Methodist, no scruple is felt nor time lost in putting one out of the church because of the doctrine of sanctification. Nineteen were expelled from one congregation. The only charge against them was that they believed in sanctification and said they enjoyed the experience.

In a Southern city we heard a man give the following remarkable testimony. He was known by the community and stood well. He was not a Methodist, but belonged to one of the largest Evangelical churches in the land. He said: "I have been turned out of my church. For twenty years I was a drinking member of that church, and have been seen repeatedly carrying a jug of whisky home in my buggy. I got drunk many times, and they never turned me out. But a year ago I was reclaimed, and soon after heard of the doctrine of sanctification. I sought it with all my heart and found it. And now with my soul full of religion my church has tried and expelled me. They could keep a drunkard on the roll, but could not stand a sanctified man."

There was not the slightest accent of bitterness in the man's voice, while his upturned face fairly shone with the light and love of God. A great thoughtfulness settled down on the audience as the fact came out for the hundredth time that card-players, theatre-goers, Sabbath breakers and even whisky drinkers can be allowed to remain in the church, while people claiming to be sanctified and living acceptably before God in thought, word and deed are thrust out of the synagogue.

To this same misunderstood and wronged class we say: "Be patient, for the coming of the Lord draweth nigh." Do not sour, no matter what may be your treatment. Be true to God, go to church, and support its institutions. Keep sweet, love everybody, say that you are sanctified and prove it by your life

As an additional thought of good cheer we call attention to the fact that the line of men and women thrust out of social and ecclesiastical circles for living close to God makes a very lengthy and glorious chain, a true Apostolical Succession.

Heading the procession is the Saviour Himself who was taken by the official members of the synagogue at Nazareth and not only thrust out, but led to the brow of the hill on which the city was built that He might be cast down and destroyed.

Paul was so frequently dragged from the Temple and synagogues and preaching places that it was with eminent fitness he said, "I die daily."

The disciples were arrested in the Temple, beaten by order of the Sanhedrim, thrust into prison, commanded to preach no more, and as the apostle said, were "counted as the filth and offscouring of the world."

Luther was a Put-out-er. So were Bunyan and Fox, and a great many others whom we might name and who, unrecognized and unappreciated in their lifetime, are now seen by the world to have been messengers of God, charged with a message, and having a dispensation of the Gospel committed unto them.

John Wesley was a Put-out-er, but not a Come-out-er. He regarded the thought of leaving his communion with pain and horror. And yet the doors of the church he loved so well were shut one after another against him all over the country. A recurring expression in his Journal is, "I was asked no more to preach in ——— church." One sermon perfectly satisfied or dissatisfied the curate or rector. Summoned before the Bishops, forbidden repeatedly by clergymen to hold meetings in their parishes, opposed by the magistrates and treated with violence by the mob, so a great portion of the life of this apostolic man was spent. Shut out from the church in which his father had served, and preaching in front of it on that father's tombstone to an audience of ten thousand people, the whole scene would make a splendid coat-of-arms for the great army of Put-out-ers who have been similarly treated for many centuries, and will continue to be so served until the coming of the Millennium.

Time would fail to tell of the spiritual Samsons, Gideons and Jepthaes, who for their faith and works' sake have been made to go forth and wander about, being destitute, despised and afflicted—but of whom it will be seen at the Last Day that the world was not worthy.

Many instances crowd on the mind, but we select

only a single case from the many. He was one of the most faithful and fearless of Methodist ministers. At home and in the social circle he was as gentle as a woman. In the pulpit the fire would fall upon him and he would speak as one inspired. Going to his circuit, his first two sermons directed upon a backslidden church were on the subjects of Intemperance and Sabbath breaking, while the third was upon Holiness. They heard him until the last topic was reached, when his leading members came together, packed his furniture and baggage in with him in a wagon, had him driven thirty miles, and dumped in the boundaries of another circuit in an adjoining county. The steward who drove the wagon groaned all the way of that thirty miles drive, while the preacher who was thus being "put out" had a constant stream of praise and hallelujahs arising in his heart and flowing from his lips every foot of the remarkable journey. What a strange duet it was that went up from the wagon that day. One man groaning, the other praising God. They never changed parts, but each one held to his own without cessation or letting down of any kind.

One more point, and we conclude the chapter. When the Pharisees and Rulers cast the man whom Christ had healed out of the synagogue, we doubt not that his heart was grieved and his mind troubled. It is no small thing to a religious nature to be Jewishly cast out, Roman Catholically excommunicated, and

Protestantly put out of the church in various ways. In this instance the man's main fault was that he had been thoroughly healed, and said that Jesus did it. He would not be confused by the cross-questioning, nor intimidated by the anger of the Jews; he firmly held his ground and said: "He hath opened mine eyes." Their answer was: "Dost thou teach us?" "and they cast him out"!

Now comes the blessed word of cheer. It is in the next verse. "Jesus heard that they had cast him out; *and when He had found him!*"

Let every man or woman who has suffered and is still suffering for Christ and the Gospel's sake, be of good cheer. If Jesus has made you whole, you owe it to Him to declare it. If such a testimony brings opposition and hardship to you in different ways; if men should thrust you out of church position and membership, there is no need for gloom or despair. Jesus sees what is going on. He knows perfectly well who is suffering for Him. He will not forget or overlook you. He who visited the three Hebrew children in the Furnace of Fire will come to you. He who hunted up the man cast out of the synagogue and interviewed him will come after you, find you, and talk with you. What a visit of glory that was in the Babylonian Furnace, and what an interview of rapture that was the excommunicated man had with the Son of God. In like manner there will be visits and interviews of such heavenly sweetness granted those who suffer for righteousness' sake in this world, that they will not feel the fire of persecution, and instead of regarding themselves as "cast out" or "put out," there will be an unutterably blissful sensation of having been "taken in" to a tenderer, holier communion with Christ and into a rest, joy and glory that seem to belong to the third and seventh heaven.

The Saviour has given the time and eternity view of such a piece of moral history. In this world He says, "Rejoice and be exceeding glad." In the world to come, "Great is your reward."

CHAPTER XVI.

SECRET SOCIETIES.

WE have been asked a number of times whether it is proper, right, and even possible for a sanctified man to belong to the various fraternities and secret societies that now fill our land and, we might say, empty our homes.

Our answer in the fear of God has been and is, that we believe the Spirit of Christ, if allowed, will lead us out of all such associations.

As for ourselves, when the light came on the subject we gave up our fraternity connection with a loss of membership fees of nearly three hundred dollars. We have never regretted the step or the loss.

In addition, we call attention to certain facts connected with these orders the consideration of which we can not but feel will convince the child of God that he should have nothing to do with them. The following argument is a part of a pamphlet we wrote on the subject several years ago:

They strike at the happiness of the home.

This is seen in the frequent and protracted absence from home they necessarily entail. It is a devoted connection which the fraternity brings about. Night after night the father and husband is away from the family circle, and this continues for years. It is in these absences of the father and husband from the family group, where they are so much needed, that we see the happiness and well-being of the home assailed.

We believe that we speak the sentiment of countless thousands of wives to-day when we say that they would far rather have the company of their husbands at home than the insurance policy connected with the fraternity at the end of their lives, if they could choose between. Ask them now, ask them anywhere, which will you have, the love and presence of your husband or the policy of $2,000 or $3,000? and the answer would roll like a tidal wave from every true-hearted woman: Give me my husband! Let me have his love and old-time devotion, and let the money go. For a woman to feel otherwise would be to transform her into a Judas.

Once there visited my study a lady of very prepossessing appearance. She told me how her life had been desolated. We shall never forget the sadness of her countenance. She said her husband was absent Monday, Tuesday, Wednesday and Thursday nights until 12 and 1 o'clock. That one night she, with a burst of grief, said to him: "My husband, suppose I would stay from you this late every night; how long would you live with me?" And he folded his arms, looked into her face a second, and replied: "Just about five minutes, madam!" And yet, what he would not endure he expected a woman to stand. The idea utterly escapes some men that there is any suffering upon the female side.

We received a letter from a prominent lady in Chicago that if printed here would make the heart ache. She attributed a broken heart and a ruined home to the influence of secret fraternities upon her husband. She said she was willing to go before any tribunal in the land, and could substantiate all she said.

The secret fraternity is rapidly becoming a club, and a place and time of convivial gathering.

No matter what the object was for which they were started, they are evidently going in this direction. You all know what a club is. We never heard of a man getting converted in a club in our life. We never heard of a man called of God to preach in a club in our life. A lady told us in New Orleans—and we will never forget her look as she said: "We women have been 'clubbed' to death." Under that witticism we read the wail of a woman's broken heart. Is it so that fraternities and societies are drifting in the direction of the club? A large collection of letters at home which we received would thoroughly answer this question.

Of course you have heard of such a thing as banquets

in connection with these fraternities and societies? Doubtless you know what happens at a banquet? In many of the fraternities there is, as far as we can hear, intoxicating liquors flowing freely. When it flows freely you know what happens. An article in a city journal said these fraternities were to build up humanity. Sometimes we have seen men coming from these banquets at a late hour, and somehow we did not feel like we were looking upon built up humanity.

These fraternities rob Christ of His glory.

We all know that benevolence, or Christian charity, as we see it in its manifold and beautiful forms, is the result of the presence and influence of Christ in the heart and in the world. We fail to see such things in the heathen world. Charity belongs to Christianity. It is the work of Christ. Now, when a man gives, and fails to acknowledge Christ in the gift, he has robbed the Son of God of his peculiar glory.

Let me illustrate: In a certain distant city there exists a newspaper that is anti-Christ, anti-religion, anti-everything that is holy. Whenever a case of public suffering comes up this paper opens its columns for contributions, and the gifts flow in. Two-thirds of the donors are Christian men and women inspired by the love of Christ; but mark you, a Christless newspaper gets the glory, and not the Saviour.

So you can take the benevolences of all these secret fraternities, and Christ is not acknowledged or thought of. One-half of the members belong to the church and give because of Christ being in their hearts and lives, but Christ does not get the glory; instead, a fraternity that may be worldly in its name and spirit, receives the honor and credit. All Christian giving when not done in the name of Jesus Christ is robbing the Son of God of His glory.

The fraternity hurts us in the matter of church attendance.

According to our observation the more faithful a man is to his lodge or fraternity the less devoted is he to his church. The claims of a secret society are only too apt to monopolize his time and energies to the slighting, and often the neglect, of the house of God. We remember a time when we had great difficulty in getting some of our members to attend an important church meeting. One could not come on Monday night on account of his lodge; a second could not appear Tuesday evening because of his fraternity meeting at that hour, and so on through the week. Each one heard a higher call than that of the church, and that higher call was his lodge.

What would you call this? Is this not rivalry to the church? Is not God grieved at such a spectacle? At one of the churches we once served there was a steward who attended one prayer-meeting in the month; the other three Wednesday evenings he was at the meetings of the different fraternities to which he belonged. How did God regard that, do you suppose? The Bible says he is a jealous God. Is there not much in such a life as this to awaken the Divine jealousy and displeasure? By and by this kind of life affects even the Sabbath attendance. The man hardens and becomes careless and indifferent, and then we miss him Sabbath nights, and finally altogether. The influence of the associations in the effect of church depreciation becomes unmistakably manifested. When God looks down and sees a church member, who is a fraternity man, failing to come to prayer-meeting and the Sunday night service, and yet never failing to be present at the meeting of his lodge, then He is bound to be grieved.

The fraternity hurts the church financially.

If you knew the whole of the matter you would be amazed. We know a church member who gives $30 a year to his fraternity, and nothing to his church. We know another who gives $120 annually to his societies, and one-fourth of this sum to his church. Still another has given lately over $500 to his fraternities and not one-tenth of that sum to his church.

In a large Western city of our country a certain fraternity met, paraded, banqueted and celebrated for three days. In that length of time more money was thus spent in eating, drinking, marching and displaying regalia finery than all the churches of that large city had given for the support and spread of the

Gospel for the previous twenty years. And yet over half of the members of that fraternity were church members.

Suppose that, instead of all this Christian money being expended for feathers, brass bands and banqueting, it had found its way in spiritual channels in all the noble enterprises of the church, and had gone toward the erection of colleges, founding of asylums and homes for the unfortunate and for the establishment of missions in heathen lands, how much better it would have been, and what a thrill of relief would have gone through the land.

Then there is the feature of the chaplaincy.

We regard this point as one of great gravity. We know that there are many excellent men in this office, and that many fraternities try to get proper men to fill the place. But it is as well known that this often fails, and that men who should never thus officiate are in the office.

How often have we seen at funerals a minister of the Gospel, whom God had called and anointed for the sacred work of the ministry, set aside as a piece of useless lumber, while a fraternity monopolized the solemn hour, and a man from the trades came forward, and although not called of God to such a work, and oftentimes not even a religious man, would conduct the religious service over the dead. Who of us can believe that this is right in the sight of God?

A gentleman, who is prominent in the fraternities, told me that he has frequently seen one of these laymen chaplains administering the oath of the order, and while doing so was partially intoxicated. Still another told me that during a visit to a large city in Kentucky he attended a meeting at a certain fraternity one night and witnessed the installation of one of the members into the office of chaplain ; and that as the Bible was handed him with the customary remarks, quite a titter ran around the room. On asking the cause of the amusement he was told that the man was guilty of a great social sin.

The effect of a sacred office thus misused and abused, and thus wrongly occupied is to bring the truth, the Bible, the ministry and the ordinances of God into contempt. It produces hardness of heart, and is bound to beget irreverence. Let the man who handles holy things be a holy man, and a man called of God and not by man. The Almighty himself has spoken here, and demands that they who bear the vessels of the Lord shall be clean. When a man opens or handles the Word of God we want him to be a man of God and called of God.

The fraternity here rushes in where angels fear to tread. They, in installing a man into a chaplaincy, have usurped the solemn, sacred work of the Holy Ghost. It would be well for them to inquire into the cause of the destruction of Dathan and Abiram and their followers. The Bible tells us that God made the earth open and swallow them up, because they took upon themselves a sacred office and work to which God had not called them.

The fraternity has captured much of our preaching talent.

This appears in two respects. We have been informed that a great per cent. of our preachers belong to secret societies. This means of course a muzzled pulpit in many quarters. Not that our preachers are afraid to declare the truth, for they are true men; but after joining a fraternity friendships are formed, kindly relations established, and it becomes difficult to speak of the evils they see.

The fraternities have captured our preachers in another way. Some of our best talent is to-day in the offices of these societies as clerks and secretaries. We believe that when God calls a man to preach the Gospel He never proposed that he should be a salaried officer in such institutions of man's organization. And although they may say they still preach here and there as occasion offers, yet it is not the preaching that God contemplated when he called them. God wants a man to swing loose free from all restrictions and limitations, and give the whole life and all the energy and time to the heaven-appointed work. This was the way that Christ preached and that the disciples labored, and it is the way for the man called of

God to preach to-day If all men who have been thus called would so devote themselves ardently to the one work of saving souls, the world would soon put on a new appearance, and take a great leap toward the millennium.

The fraternity is used by many as a substitute for the church.

How often have you heard men say about Masonry that it was as good as the church; that they wanted no other church! But you have got to remember that Jesus Christ did not found it, nor did He join it, nor did He endorse it. Christ founded the church and told us to come into that. When men found an institution and tell us that it is as good as the church, we think those men are in danger. We would not stay a moment in an institution if its teaching and spirit would produce a feeling of that kind among its members.

Nothing has so powerfully convinced us of the dangerous power of these fraternities and their actual rivalship of the church as the publicly uttered threat of some church members, that they would quit the church if their pastor said aught against their Order.

What a state of mind and things does this reveal. These men and women would cease to listen to a man called of God to preach, and would dissolve their connection with a Divine institution if a man should open his lips in warning and rebuke against a human institution! Certainly these societies have encroached upon the feelings and judgments of men, to thus plant them in antagonism to the servants and church of the Son of God.

Many of these fraternities are striking at the sanctity of the Sabbath.

We speak of a vast number of fraternities, benevolent and otherwise, that fill the land to-day. In some cities we could name, much of the Sabbath-breaking is done by societies and fraternities—in parades, processions, picnics and excursions. God's holy day is made to look like a holiday. How the heart has been pained as we have seen them on the Sabbath with fluttering flags and musical instruments, accompanied by the usual street crowd of men and boys, pushing their way to the point of destination. Many a time we have been kept awake on Sunday night hours, by the sounds of music and dancing that flowed from one of these fraternity halls near our home.

Active membership in these fraternities will certainly harm the spirituality of a Christian.

Whom do you find comprising these fraternities? We grant you many excellent persons. But besides these there is a host of men who are unbelievers and haters of God and the Bible. With these you are thrown as companions and friends. They create an atmosphere; form an influence. You breathe the atmosphere and feel the influence. The effect will be to lower the tone of your religious life. Why does the Bible say, "Be not unequally yoked together with unbelievers"? Why does God say, "Blessed is the man that walketh not in the counsel of the ungodly"? and why does he say, "Come out from among them, O my people"? All this is simply the recognition of the fact that the religious life and character is affected by its associations, and that there is danger here, and great danger, for the people of God.

In all of the fraternities and in all the degrees of Masonry under the Knights Templar, the name of Jesus Christ is omitted.

This to my mind is the gravest fact of all. The Saviour's name is not known in them. If you doubt, get hold of the rituals and read and seek in vain. Listen to the public prayers. Go to the funeral services and listen for the name of Jesus Christ. You will listen in vain. Now, then, we do not care to be connected with any order on earth that fails to recognize the Son of God. Christ says: "He that is ashamed of me, of him will I be ashamed." "He that denies me before men, him will I deny." This applies to an individual and to an institution as well. We can not belong to a society or fraternity that is ashamed of the Lord, or that to please men will leave out His blessed name; therefore have we dissolved our connection with all fraternities forever. With nothing but the kindest personal feelings to its members, with only kindly remembrances of individuals, yet we are done with the system itself.

There is no absolute necessity for these societies.

If you examine the social feature, history proves it is not the best. The best development of the social nature is not obtained by the separation of the sexes, but by their being drawn together. Club life is the confirmation of this statement.

As for the benevolent feature, we say that while good has been done, we verily believe that if God's people would take the contributions and turn them into the channels marked out by the Bible and church, greater good would be done at less expense and with greater glory to Christ.

We can not see the necessity of these orders. We got along without them for ages and ages, and we believe we can get along without them for ages and ages to come. Do not forget that when Christ established an institution that is to take this world, He did not found a secret fraternity, but a church that is open as the heavens in its sacraments, ordinances, teachings and meetings.

Let me exhort you, my brethren, to give up the fraternity, and instead stand by your home and that little woman there whom you call your wife. You have not a better friend on earth than that wife of yours. She left everything to follow you in life. She gave up father and mother and a comfortable home. You have not been to her what you should have been, and what you promised when she stood as a bride by your side and looked up in her helplessness to you. The light you notice is going out of her eye, the spring from her step, and she is getting prematurely old. Go back to her and spend the evenings with her as you used to do. Pay her the old-time attentions, and before a week the light will begin to come back to the eye, the color steal into her cheek. she will fasten a bit of ribbon or a knot of flowers in her hair and be like her old-time self.

The children all love you. There is no other group on earth that loves you like the family group. When sickness and trouble come, and you stagger home, you find it out. What do those men down the street with whom you talk and go so much—what do they care for you? So look to your family. Cultivate the home circle.

When your wife is dead you will remember the loneliness of her life, produced by your attendance night after night upon these fraternities. When that little boy of yours is dead, and sleeps in his grave on the hillside, they will tell you then how much he missed you in the evenings you were gone, and how he talked about you and waited, hoping you would return before he fell asleep.

How bitterly you will feel all this when the time comes. I once saw a man whose wife had died. He did not awaken to her value until then. His heart was broken. He had just found out that he had an angel for a wife. He did not know it until he heard the rush of her wings through the blue space to the throne of God, and then cried, "My God, she is gone!" O, brother, come back to her, come back and spend the evenings at home! What a time you can have for reading; what sweet music you can have; what romps with the children; what a sweet domestic scene we have before us now! And if there is any evening that the house of God calls you out, come and bring them all with you. How different this is from the fraternities. You can not take them with you there. Go rather to the place where you can hear words of grace from the pulpit; go where the soul is fed; go and assemble with God's people and not with worldly people; and go where you will be fitted for a higher, nobler and eternal life.

Stand by the church rather than any fraternity on the earth. Stand by the church, for it is of God. It cost the precious blood of our Saviour. It is the one institution that is going to survive the flames of the last day. When the fire burns around the whole world, and the flames leap from the heart of the earth to the tops of the mountains and swallow up all things in a final destruction—then every earthly institution shall sink into the common ruin with no hope of resurrection. Fraternities and earthly orders will go down forever, but the church, the church of our Lord, purified and redeemed, shall rise above flames, and far above the stars, and be landed in the presence of our God forever. Stand by the Saviour, the Lord Jesus Christ. He gave His own heart's blood for you, now do you stand by Him? You will want Him to be with you in the dying hour. You will want Him to be your friend when the final day of judgment comes. Make Him your friend now and say, "O Lord, I am yours from to-day in all things, under all circumstances, and at all times, forever and forever."

CHAPTER XVII.

SIDETRACKS.

IF there is any man whom the devil fears and hates above other men it is the sanctified or fire-baptized Christian. He knows that in him he has an unrelenting, uncompromising foe, and one who having the enduement of power will do him and his kingdom more harm in a year than an hundred other persons put together who know not the "mystery of the Gospel" and possess not the "secret of the Lord."

The Adversary seemed to pay but little attention to the disciples prior to their reception of the baptism of the Holy Ghost. But when the holy fire fell upon them and they flew with shining faces, liberated tongues and irresistible lives everywhere preaching the Gospel with the Holy Ghost sent down from heaven, then he and the dark phalanxes of hell arose and moved after and upon them, so that from that time their history, though filled with glorious victories for Christ, was lined with dungeons, scourgings, stonings, and dreadful persecutions, while some kind of martyrdom terminated the career of every one. As he could not cool their zeal, nor make them sin, he killed them one by one; Paul being beheaded, Peter crucified head downward, Matthew skinned alive, James knocked from an high place and beat to death with fuller's clubs in the streets of Jerusalem, and each one ending life in some ghastly way conceived by Satanic hate and executed by human agency in league with the devil.

To this day the great Adversary hates and dreads a fire-baptized man. He has no alarm and concerns himself but little over the multitude of Christians who spend most of their time in the Round House receiving or waiting for repairs. But let one of them obtain the Baptism of the Holy Ghost and fire and be transformed in a flash from a condition of helplessness into a great spiritual locomotive full of divine life and power, heading for heaven, and carrying a long train of souls with them; and then full of fury he plots and endeavors from that moment the ruin of that same useful life.

Of course, he would prefer to destroy outright such foes to himself and such hinderers of his work. He would like to bring about a collision, or derail such a life and cause it to plunge down the bank to ruin. If he can not do this, then he tries to steal away the fire, the secret of the man's power. If still he does not succeed, his next and more successful effort is to sidetrack the man. This is done in one of several ways, and that it is done we need only look about us. As in the railroad world there is one main track and many sidetracks, so it seems in the spiritual life. We have been astonished at the number of different sidelines into which Satan has switched off some of the servants of God. In some cases the engine is "dead," as the engineers call it; the fire is out, and the man once a power is now idle and inactive in the great work in which he once gladly and mightily engaged, and in which hundreds of his brethren are still rushing. In other cases, the spiritual steam is up, and the man is backing up and down with considerable whistling and ringing of bells, but he gets nowhere. Everybody can see he is sidetracked.

We mention several of these tracks. One is

SIN.

It is noticeable that Satan in trying to get a Christian to sin, and so end his life in failure and ruin, uses the two methods of Presumption and Despair upon him; and they follow in the order mentioned. The first onset is made with the whisper, "Oh, it is a little thing; no harm will come of it; it can be rectified." The second assault is a wail, "You are undone; there is no hope for you."

In a word, as some one has said, he presents sin to you at first as such a narrow stream that if you go across it you can easily step back. But when the sin has been committed, suddenly under a glare of horrific light the little stream is seen to have widened into a dark, roaring ocean that seems to be bottomless and shoreless.

The Adversary well knows the effect of this last impression or revelation made to the soul; he is confident the man will be paralyzed with despair, and failing to see the grace and power of the Atonement across that turbulent flood he has stretched before the spiritual vision, will sooner or later, going from sin to sin, finally sink into the depths of ruin.

The devil knows well the constitution of the soul. He has studied the human spirit long enough to understand it. He knows that a sense of lost cleanness, lost virtue, lost holiness is the sharpest and most unendurable of pangs; and so if upon this natural distress he can graft the spirit of hopelessness his end is accomplished. The man is sidetracked!

Alas, that such cases have been seen. Men whose voice and face and presence were sources of inspiration to God's people, and whose deeds and life struck terror to the heart of hell, now sidetracked through a single act of wrong.

We can never forget the profound impression once made on an audience by a preacher who was describing the fall of Judas. Two steps of the ruin portrayed by two scenes in the man's life, and all but acted by the speaker, seemed to bring the congregation into a condition of breathless awe. One scene showed the devil putting the *thought* of the Betrayal into the heart of Judas. The Scripture describes this in the words, "The devil having put it into his heart to betray

Him." The attitude of surprise on the part of Satan as Judas, one of the twelve, received and cherished the thought was a sermon in itself. The awful triumph on the devil's face, his diabolical malice, his withering sneer, "Why, he allows the temptation to remain in his heart! He cherishes the thought!" altogether made this part of the apostle's fall one of unspeakable dreadfulness.

The second scene revealed *the devil entering into Judas*. The Scripture for this being found in the words, "Satan having entered into him."

See the difference: In the first scene Satan is beheld putting the *thought* of evil in the man's mind, while in the second he brings *himself* into the man and takes possession.

The preacher threw a book on a certain part of the platform, and after a minute of silent looking in that direction, followed the book up with himself. The two steps were thus incarnated before the eyes of the people.

The evil thought is the forerunner of the devil; for Satan knows that if a Christian will allow the evil thought he will in time allow the originator of the temptation to come in. The thought of sin is sent to prepare the way for the complete admission of the Adversary.

So the attitude of Satan near the tempted soul, watching with astonishment, as well as infernal glee, the entertainment of an evil thought by an apostle of Jesus Christ or any once devoted child of God, fairly awes the mind with the fact of the moral crises in men's history, the dreadful danger of the soul, and the gloomy tragedies taking place in the spiritual life.

The ultimate possession of the man by the devil, and his going out in the night to commit his deed of darkness, is like the continued tolling of a funeral knell as the last spadeful of earth is thrown on the grave, like a curtain falling on a suicide, or night coming down upon a ghastly, lonely murder.

A second sidetrack is readily seen in the word

IMPRUDENCE.

There are some of God's people, who from lack of proper early training, have been known to do things innocently that nevertheless were hurtful to them.

Then there are true Christian men so conscious of their own integrity before God, and faithfulness to men, that their very realization of a character that can stand tests and remain true, may create a fearlessness and boldness, and perhaps at times an ignoring of proprieties and appearances, that if persisted in is certain to bring lasting harm to the influence of the individual, whether he be layman or preacher.

There are certain social customs and demands that are as unbending as the laws on the two tables of stone. If a man heedlessly and repeatedly breaks them, he himself will be broken. If he ignores them, he himself will be ignored. If he sets them aside, the public will set him aside.

Some very melancholy things could be written under this head in the way of illustration, but we are confident that the warning alone of the danger is best and will be sufficient. Suffice it to say that numbers of times we have observed human lights that had been ignited by the Lord, and that seemed for awhile to attract every eye, and then began to pale little by little, and finally disappeared altogether. The explanation sometimes is that the people have seen certain things in the life which made them unwilling to follow such a standard bearer. The man was sidetracked by the devil through acts of imprudence.

A third sidetrack is seen in the word

HABITS.

We do not refer to what some would call personal eccentricities or mannerisms. One of the deeply interesting features of sanctification is the way it brings out the peculiar gifts and individuality of the person receiving the blessing. The purifying of the heart, the empowering of the Holy Ghost, the deliverance from man-fear, the delightful consciousness of liberty. and the realization of a child-like nature, all received in sanctification, is the explanation and philosophy of the strangely marked individual manifestations so noticeable in the Holiness movement. We do not wish to see this changed. It is a part of the excellence and power of the blessing.

By "habits" we do not refer to the dress question and to the way some people keep, or do not keep, their bodies. Although it does seem to the writer that if any one on earth should be scrupulously clean in body and neat in attire it should be a man or woman claiming the blessing of sanctification. The profession of a pure heart, while carrying around a neglected body, clothed in untidy garments does not sound well, nor look well, and will not take well.

Men may affect to despise these things, but sooner or later their own personal untidiness or uncleanliness will sidetrack them. Such persons themselves are the last to see it, but others see it.

We recall a scene beheld by us once at Conference. It has often recurred to the memory. It lasted only a minute, but it had vividness for coloring and the clear-cut lines of chain-lightning for its edges and frame-work. A preacher claiming the blessing of holiness stopped to speak to another minister of the Conference who did not believe in the doctrine or experience. The latter was puffing a cigar. The former sported no cigar but wore a soiled shirt.

"Brother," said the sanctified brother, "take that dirty cigar out of your mouth."

"Brother," replied the Zinzendorfian, "take that unclean shirt and collar off your body."

Here was a Grant for a McPherson and a Roland for an Oliver.

Let it be understood that we are not pleading for fashionable attire, but for physical cleanliness and certain proprieties of dress. We may claim to have reached a point of superiority to these things, but it will eventually end in a sidetrack. We have gifted men to-day in the Gospel work whose influence would penetrate into circles that they have not yet reached if they would dress less oddly and become as inconspicuous in their attire in one way as they demand of their congregations in another.

He who commanded the Jews to wash frequently, and was careful that His ministering servants in the Temple should wear white and spotless linen has not changed His mind.

By "habits" we refer mainly to the indulgence of artificial tastes and appetites, such as the use of tobacco in snuff-dipping, smoking and chewing.

We do not mean to say that a man can not have religion if he has the tobacco habit; yet confess to surprise at his saying that he *enjoys* religion while in the indulgence of what is clearly a lust of the flesh. It seems so clearly opposed by the teaching of the Bible, and so contrary to the mind, spirit and pure self-denying, cross-bearing life of Christ, that we have often wondered how one could do this thing and call himself a follower of Jesus.

It did not require sanctification to make the writer give up the tobacco habit, to which he had been devoted as a smoker for years. A good case of regeneration settled the question and ended its practice forever with him. He found the surrender necessary to the enjoyment of that communion he craved with his Lord. Other regenerated people seem to have found a broader and easier way, but the author of this book could never find it. But, then, he did not want to find it: the narrow way of the Gospel was very attractive to him and eminently satisfying.

Because of the facts stated it has been a matter of great wonder to us to hear of, and several times to see, people who claimed to be sanctified and yet used tobacco. The incongruity of the profession of a clean heart with an unclean habit at once impresses the reader. And when in addition we note the expensiveness of the practice, the destruction in this way of God's money, the injury it works upon nerve, brain and body, and finally the utter un-Christlikeness of the indulgence we marvel that a man would have the face to stand up and claim holiness with such a background against him as we have drawn.

Of course they defend themselves and the habit. Even the heathen take up for their gods. So some say they use it "*medicinally*"! And as we have gone over the entire country we have been astonished to find how many healing virtues is possessed by tobacco not known by scientists and not put down in *Materia Medica* volumes.

Others ashamed of the medicine dodge say they use it because they are "free." Religious liberty is the fig leaf this time. But the spiritually thoughtful see that "freedom" in these cases is nothing but "license."

We once knew an old gentleman who belonged to our church, who claimed the blessing of sanctification and yet was addicted to the use of tobacco. He was very voluble at class-meeting and had a way of dry shouting. Many noticed the hollowness of the voice in these mechanical vociferations. And one remarkable fact was impressed upon us that not a soul in the church, not even the sanctified people, believed he had the blessing. So the conclusion was forced on the mind that if a man can use tobacco and remain sanctified, yet such is the effect of the habit on the minds of others that no one but himself will believe he has the blessing.

We have known several other individuals who claimed to have a clean heart back of an unclean mouth, and we have noticed that without a single exception they were without spiritual power. There was a notable lack of joy in the experience, freedom in the life, unction in the speech and **power in the life.**

We also find that men will not listen to or be guided by them. They claim purity with an unclean habit ; they say they have crucified the flesh with all its appetites and lusts, and yet are here pandering to it ; they insist they love men with a perfect love, while they spit enough money on the ground or puff enough into the air to keep bodies from starvation and souls from hell. They say they follow Christ and take Him as an example, when no one will believe for a moment that the Saviour would be guilty of a practice that is unclean, expensive, hurtful to the body, unpleasant and sickening to innocent parties and always to be condemned as a bad example to the young.

The whole thing is too inconsistent. The testimony and life are too unlike and contradictory. Men will not believe in nor follow them, and they will find after awhile they are switched off. They are still smoking, but they are not running, or drawing anything. They are sidetracked !

A fourth sidetrack is,—

The magnifying of a single feature of the Blessing or Work of Sanctification above the whole.

We have all seen this mistake. The characters who made it ran well for awhile and then switched off on some issue or question connected with the grace, of secondary importance.

We firmly believe in dressing to please Christ, and are as firmly convinced of the instantaneous healing power of Christ in answer to prayer and faith. We have not only seen it take place in others, but felt it in our own body. But just as steadfastly do we believe that these questions should not be magnified above the greater blessing of a pure heart. It is vastly more important that a man be made to see the need of, and possess a sanctified soul than to believe in a certain kind of attire and obtain a healed body. The Bible teaches this, and men of common sense feel it to be true.

Now, then, let a man instead of presenting a full-orbed holiness go to stressing a single feature of it and he is certain to be sidetracked. Men will not go to hear a person striking at one evil in the spiritual life all the time, or exalting one feature of the blessing at the expense of the others.

When a body of Christians cease presenting the great subjects of Inbred Sin, the Baptism with the Holy Ghost, the Necessity of the Blessing, the Power of the Blessing, and go to fighting feathers, making it the main subject matter of each discourse and conversation, they have become sidetracked.

There is something better than combating the symptoms of a disease. The Bible strikes at the malady itself, and lo! the symptoms all disappear. When the soul is made to see Inbred Sin, and then the beauty of holiness; when it gets rid of the first and possesses the second, every questionable thing will be put off the body and out of the life. It is not the external thrashing of the winds of March that makes the last dead leaves fall off the branches of the trees to which they have clung all winter; but the rich, vigorous sap of springtime, which coursing up the tree trunk and flowing out into every limb, branch and twig, fairly pushes off and flings down upon the ground these yellow and untimely flutterers. So it is not so much pulpit thrashing and pew abuse that causes people to give up personal adornments, as the rich life of Christ stealing into every part of the soul, body and life ; and lo ! as the antlers drop from the head of the deer, and the skin is cast from the snake, everything that is worldly and carnal will be flung off from the individual who is filled with the Holy Ghost.

We were once much impressed by a remark made by Amanda Smith in regard to being switched off from the main track of Holiness; she said in substance : "You think you are all right because you keep moving ; but you are moving on a sidetrack, and as certain as you live you will yet strike a ' Bumper,' and the end of your life-work and usefulness will come."

We have only to look about us to see the truth of that speech. The man who allows himself to be absorbed in some secondary matter, which becomes a pet subject and measure and actually eclipses greater truths, is certain to strike the " Bumper " at last, and it will be in the shape of Public Opinion. People will not listen long to such a man and such a one-sided teaching. They will see that he is off the main track, and not desiring to be like him, they leave him to his short runs, steam whistle fussiness and to the immovable Bumper at last.

The fifth sidetrack is

ERRONEOUS TEACHING.

There has always been a great amount of this. Paul warns against it, and so does every true lover of God and souls.

There is a wonderful readiness to hear among people. The Athenian spirit for something new is also still abroad. There are people with itching ears, and there are tongues that love to scratch such itching ears. We know of good people who are ready to swallow down everything that comes along in a doctrinal way. The newer and stranger the teaching the more they seem to relish it.

This being the case, there is always an open field for wrong and mistaken teachers. The following that seems to be easily created by any with any doctrine, operates as a double deception to teacher and taught. They both look upon it as the seal of heaven upon the movement, and as the earnest of the general victory which they feel is certain to come.

But such men soon run their course. Error is

bound to be discovered at last, the following falls away, and the teacher is left sidetracked.

We remember once to have read that Satan can deceive some people a part of the time, and others most of the time, but he can not deceive everybody all the time.

So with the false or mistaken teacher. He can influence some men, but not all men; and he may affect many men a little while, but he can not do so all the while. The truth will come up at last. Error of heart, inconsistency of life, and extravagance of doctrinal statement are certain to be found out, and the teacher's work is over forever. Men will not follow him any more.

We have all beheld this in various religious movements, and in the Holiness cause as well. We have observed men whose hearts were good, but whose heads were not equal to their hearts, go off into fanciful interpretations of Scripture, insisting that an experience of their own was proof of a doctrine and so taught, and exhorted all to follow them. But what they thought was a headlight, proved to be a switch-light, and teacher and taught found themselves at last off the maintrack on a sidetrack.

A man who although sanctified has taught erroneously, finds it an impossibility to get the people to trust him again as a teacher. They feel that as once before he could not tell the difference between the false and true, he is not to be relied on now. That which he calls the Star of Bethlehem may be a will-o'-the-wisp light and land them all sooner or later in a bog of error and slough of despair.

The man who suffers himself to be betrayed into wrong teaching, will be a sidetracked man. It will be a gradual thing, for trains get on a sidetrack slowly, but it will be done. Reports will be taken, letters will pass, communities will become fearful and invitations will cease. By and by the Bumper is reached and the man is sidetracked.

Some of this erroneous teaching is known to all and need not be mentioned here. We content ourselves in this concluding point with reference to

THE THIRD BLESSING ERROR.

This teaching being unscriptural is destined to go down; but owing to the fact that some good people are very credulous, and that many excellent individuals have an imperfect knowledge of the Bible, there may be always some who will adhere to it as Gospel truth.

The Holiness people as headed by such men as Wesley, Clarke and Benson, of the old world, and by Asbury, Inskip, and a host of others in this country; and with such journals as *The Witness*, of Boston, the *Standard*, of Philadelphia, and the *Pentecostal Herald*, of Louisville; and with multiplied thousands and tens of thousands of level-headed and sound-hearted people in the ranks—all stand for two works of grace in the soul, regeneration and sanctification. The first preceded by repentance and faith, and the second followed by an endless growth in grace. Two works of grace, the first being pardon and life to the soul; the second purity and power; this last being wrought in the heart by the Son of God when He baptizes the believer with the Holy Ghost and fire. Peter said it "purified" and Christ said it "empowered." After its reception the Saviour said the disciples could go anywhere, preaching, teaching and prevailing; and they did go forth to the uttermost parts of the earth and had victory everywhere.

This summary above is the belief of the regular, Old Guard, unswitched-off Holiness people.

The brethren who advocate the third blessing say that after we are sanctified and have had the Baptism of the Holy Ghost there is a Baptism of Fire as a third work of grace or blessing. They affirm it is to be sought just as the Baptism of the Holy Ghost or sanctification is obtained. That when received, the indication of its reception is a certain fullness of love, knowledge and power in the soul, and a certain tingling sensation in the body.

To the Third Blessing view we offer the following objections:

First, it makes Christ to have two Baptisms for

the soul instead of one, as taught by the Word of God.

The Baptism of the Holy Ghost is one thing with them, and the Baptism of Fire another. To the question, What is this Fire but the Holy Ghost? there is bound to be embarrassment. The Bible says, "Our God is a consuming fire," and if they claim the "fire" to be different from God, then are we baptized with something other than God, and hence less than God. This being the case, how can the Third Blessing be superior? The Bible recognizes but one spiritual baptism. Paul distinctly says there is "one baptism," and the wise scholars have long ago seen from the connection that he was not speaking of water-baptism.

The words of John the Baptist teach one baptism by the Son of God. "I indeed baptize you with water . . but He shall baptize you with the Holy Ghost and [with] fire." The word in the brackets is not in the original.

Any one studying this verse will see there is but one baptism meant. If there was a first baptism to be followed later by a second the language would have to be changed.

The argument made on the two words, "Holy Ghost and fire," if admitted, could be made to prove that there are two births at regeneration. It will be remembered by the reader that Jesus said to Nicodemas, "Except a man be born of water and [of] the Spirit he can not enter into the kingdom of God." The word in brackets is not in the original. According to the Third Blessing logic here are two distinct births, while we all know there is but one birth. There is a birth of the flesh and a birth of the Spirit. There is but one birth after the natural birth, for Jesus said, "Ye must be born *again*," not born twice more.

Where does the water birth come in and what does it accomplish? Does not any one see that it is but the church rite, the external sign of an inward and spiritual grace? The water stands for the washing of regeneration, just as the visible flames of fire falling on the disciples were announcers and declarers of the inward holy, sanctifying fire, with which Christ was then baptizing them.

We look in vain for this Second Baptism of fire in the Word of God. When the disciples received the Baptism of the Holy Ghost tongues of fire fell and sat upon their heads. This is the only time that there was a visible flame. We never heard any one in our lives say that this cloven flame which moved upon their heads like celestial plumes did any spiritual work in their hearts. It was a divine external manifestation and attestation. The real work was going on inside the disciples with the Holy Ghost as a consuming fire.

The Word of God and that scene at Pentecost agree in showing that Christ has one Baptism.

The language of Scripture is "born of the flesh," "born of the Spirit," and "baptized with the Holy Ghost and [with] fire." One birth of the flesh, one birth of the Spirit, and one baptism with the Holy Ghost.

A second objection to the Third Blessing view is that it belittles the Baptism of the Holy Ghost, or work of sanctification.

Any one can see that if a third blessing called the Baptism of Fire is needed for the soul after sanctification, then the Baptism of the Holy Ghost did not accomplish a perfect cleansing and empowering work.

Let us see what is the Bible and historic presentation of the Baptism of the Holy Ghost.

As the reader knows, it is called "Christ's Baptism," the one prophesied for ages and received by the disciples on the Day of Pentecost. You remember how it fired and filled them. This same blessing was said by Peter the morning it came upon him, to be for others as well as for the apostles. It was soon after obtained by Samaritans, Romans and Greeks, Paul asking the last named the question, "Have ye received the Holy Ghost since ye believed?" It was this that many in Wesley's time sought for and obtained, and under its inspiration and force swept the land for God as the disciples had done before under the same mighty grace. It was this that kindled John S. Inskip and sent him flying in every direction as a burning apostle of holiness. The same blessing came upon the soul of the writer eight years ago, and since that hour he has labored unweariedly for Christ, with a love for God and man that nothing has been able to shake, cool or sour. Under this crowning grace we have got to know what sixty and an hundred-fold mean in Christian labor and fruit.

It is this blessing that is the origin, sweetness, glory and power of the Holiness movement, which is going everywhere to-day.

Now, as I have taken note of all these things, and remembered that Christ called it Enduement of Power, telling the disciples not to leave Jerusalem until they received it; and as Peter said it "purified the heart by faith," it is not to be wondered at that we publicly asked the question, "What can be greater than the Baptism with the Holy Ghost?" We see what it did for the apostles, for the Wesleys, and for us to-day, and the question was as natural as true.

It was answered by a third blessing brother in these words: "I answer emphatically there is. All the fulness of the blessed Holy Trinity—the Father and the Son and the Holy Ghost experienced as a divine verity in my soul, manifesting and revealing themselves to my innermost consciousness as distinct personalities and abiding continually within me—is greater and more wonderful to me than simply the fulness of the Holy Ghost. This indwelling and bursting forth in three-fold fiery glory of the Triune God is what I mean by the Baptism of Fire; and this the Lord vouchsafes to me."

According to this brother's idea, the Baptism with the Holy Ghost brings in the fulness of the Holy Ghost, and the Baptism of Fire ushers in the fulness of the Father and the Son.

He gives no Scripture for this remarkable assertion. In fact, there is none. In absence of Scripture for this remarkable assertion, he makes the statement that he and others have the experience.

This sounds very well, but there are many people who prefer to follow the Word and want a thus saith the Lord before they will believe there is a third work of grace or blessing.

In utter refutation of his idea and to show that the Baptism of the Holy Ghost does bring in the fulness of the Trinity, we call attention to the fourteenth chapter of John, where the Saviour is speaking of the coming blessing of Pentecost or Baptism of the Holy Ghost. He says the Spirit is now "with you," but "shall be *in* you" and to "abide forever." He then adds in further description of the blessing that "We (my Father and I) will come unto him and make our abode with him."

Paul also settles the question that sanctification brings in "*all* the fulness of God" in his prayer for the Christian Church. The expressions, "strengthened with might," "Christ dwell in your hearts," "rooted and grounded in love," all show what he is referring to, and what has been felt by every truly sanctified man. Any one can see that these are not different blessings but parts, or features, of the one great blessing, the crowning description of which the apostle gives in the next breath, "that ye might be filled with all the fulness of God."

Here is the portrayal of the second work of grace by the Saviour and Paul. The former makes the Baptism with the Holy Ghost to bring in the Father and Son into the soul, and the latter calls it being filled with all the fulness of God. Can any one see the need of a third work of grace?

One birth of the Spirit, one Baptism with the Holy Ghost, and many blessings and refreshings from the presence of the Lord. This seems to be the Biblical order. We do not believe it can be improved.

A third objection to the Third Blessing view is that it leaves Inbred Sin in the heart after sanctification or the Baptism of the Holy Ghost.

The advocates of the third work in denial insist that they simply contend for an "empowering" in the Baptism of Fire.

This position we easily overthrow by the words of Jesus, who said to his disciples, "Ye shall be baptized with the Holy Ghost not many days hence," and two verses further on adds, "Ye shall receive *power* after that the Holy Ghost is come upon you."

Here not a word is said about a Baptism of Fire, but power was to come from the Baptism of the Holy Ghost. With that "pow r" and "baptism" they went unto the uttermost parts of the earth. They were completely purified and qualified for Christian service, and needed no third work of grace.

Now, then, to say that after the Baptism of the Holy Ghost there is needed a Baptism of Fire, is to teach that the nature or principle of sin is left in the heart. For if, as the Bible says, the Baptism of the Holy Ghost empowers, what is the Baptism of Fire to do, but to purify?

The very insistence upon the necessity of a Baptism of Fire for the soul after sanctification shows remaining uncleanness. Fire destroys and cleanses. This is its peculiar power and work. Coming down upon the sanctified soul then, to do anything it must find something to destroy and something to cleanse, and what could that be but sin?

So here by the Third Blessing view we are taught by the faithfulness of Bible figures that the Baptism of the Holy Ghost did not remove inbred sin, and that a sanctified man is not sanctified.

Sanctify means to make pure, to make holy. But if we have to seek a Baptism of Fire subsequent to our sanctification then something is left in us that is unclean and to be destroyed, and so we are not sanctified or pure at all. How the Bible upsets all these wrong notions and false reasoning. Peter, in speaking of the Baptism of the Holy Ghost, said that by it the "hearts were purified." Certainly there is no room for Inbred Sin in the soul after that.

It is evident to the thoughtful that to insist upon a Baptism of Fire to be sought for by sanctified people is by an unavoidable Scriptural logic to compel such people to admit they have in them Inbred Sin.

It is also remarkable that such reasoners have unconsciously joined hands with Meyer, Murray, Moody, and all the Northfield School, who teach that sanctification or the Baptism with the Holy Ghost is nothing but an anointing for service of the regenerated soul, or, truly speaking, a Greasing of the Old Man.

God does not want the Old Man anointed. It is not oil that he needs but fire! He needs to be killed not anointed.

Such superficial views of the work of Christ, such a belittling of Christ's Baptism with the Holy Ghost can not but do harm and does do harm.

A fourth objection to the Third Blessing view is that it mars what we call the dual symmetry of the Bible.

The double work of salvation is clearly taught in Scripture. Pardon and Purity are held up all through the Book. Peace is connected with Pardon, and Power with Purity. The Apostle Paul writes to Titus about the double work of grace in the words,

"He saved us by the washing of regeneration *and* the renewing of the Holy Ghost which He shed on us abundantly through Jesus Christ our Saviour." We see it shadowed forth in the two sin-offerings, the two rooms in the Tabernacle and the two angels in the Holy of Holies. We hear it sung in the grand old hymn:

"Be of sin the DOUBLE cure,
Save from wrath and make me pure."

According to the Third Blessing view there should be another clause to the verse in Titus, a third sin-offering, a third room in the Tabernacle, three angels in the Holiest, while the hymn should read,

"Be of sin the TRIPLE cure."

A fifth objection to the Third Blessing teaching is that it is unscriptural.

We can not find anywhere in the Bible where people sought and found the Baptism of Fire as a third blessing.

The only time it is mentioned it is seen to be identical with the Baptism of the Holy Ghost as it fell on the disciples.

In Samaria the converts of Philip, under the teaching of Peter and John, received the Baptism of the Holy Ghost.

Cornelius, the Roman Centurion, obtained the Baptism of the Holy Ghost while Peter was preaching. There is no mention of a third blessing after this.

When Paul came to Ephesus and found certain disciples he did not say, "Have ye received the Baptism of Fire which ushers in the fulness of the Father and the Son?" but his words were, "Have ye received the Holy Ghost since ye believed?"

No mention is made here or elsewhere about a distinct Baptism of Fire, because the Baptism of the Holy Ghost is a Baptism of Fire. He who gets the one obtains the other; these two are never separated. Just as the sea of glass is permeated with fire, so the Baptism of the Holy Ghost is one of fire. Whoever obtains Christ's Baptism with the Holy Ghost gets the fire. Hallelujah! when it came upon us eight years ago, it was fire! We felt it from head to foot, and while it burned in the soul we felt it tingling to the very extremities of the body. We have never felt the need of a third blessing or work of grace, and looking into the Bible we can find none promised. Christ's Baptism with the Holy Ghost and fire we want and need, and all any one needs. Hallelujah! it can be obtained.

A sixth objection to the Third Blessing view is that when accepted it starts a line of other works that are simply endless.

We have observed that when men depart from strict Scripture teaching, they do not rest in the new error, but go on to others. Our readers who have read church history will remember that when the Catholic Church added a third sacrament to the two taught by the Bible, it was not long before they had seven! So will it be here.

We know a lady who became dissatisfied with her sanctified life, and sought what she called the Baptism of Love. She ran on that for a few months and then claimed to have received the Baptism of Power. After that she obtained two other kind of Baptisms, whereupon we prayed in our heart that she might receive the Baptism of Common Sense, but up to the latest accounts she has not yet received it.

In a town in one of our Southern States, a gentleman who has gone off into the Third Blessing movement, has published in a paper the epochs of his Christian life. The almanac feature is remarkable:

Converted—1870.

Sanctified—1876.

Received the Holy Ghost—1880.

Baptized with Fire—1897.

He had two other divine works on the list which we can not recall. It is evident that he is not done. He will go on multiplying and inventing as Fancy suggests, or some wandering teacher should present to the mind, until he himself shall finally became bewildered and know not where he is.

Oh, how we need not only the sincerity of Jesus Christ but His simplicity.

To the question, How can we account for good people falling into such an error? our reply is,—

First, some who never had been sanctified, received it at last and called it the Baptism of Fire or the third blessing. They had taken the blessing by faith but had not received the witness. They were living clean and quiet lives and thought they were sanctified, when they were not. In this condition being stirred up by faithful preaching they sought ardently for what was called the "Fire," and this time complying with every condition and taking no denial, down came the mighty Baptism with the Holy Ghost, the holy fire flashed all through their spirits, and they thought they had received the third blessing, when for the first time they had obtained the second blessing, or were sanctified.

Another explanation is that some sanctified people lose their power, the fire goes down, and the blessing leaks out. We have known such, who instead of confessing their loss and seeking to be renewed, would come to the altar for the Baptism of Fire or the Third Blessing. What they needed to do was to make a wholesome confession to the audience and go down on their knees as a backslider from holiness. What they needed to ask for was not the third blessing, but the Second Blessing restored. Not to get new fire, but the old fire back in their souls.

One thing is certain that according to the words of

Christ the Baptism with the Holy Ghost brings "enduement of power," according to Peter the heart is "purified," and according to Luke, who saw it, the "fire" comes at the same instant with the Baptism of the Holy Ghost.

If sanctification or the Baptism with the Holy Ghost is not "power" and "purity" and "fire," it is nothing, and the Word of God is not to be relied on, and the experience of multiplied thousands of truly sanctified people living in all ages and countries are not to be regarded a moment.

Thank God for sanctification, for the Baptism with the Holy Ghost and with fire, all three in one. He who gets one, gets all. For him there is no third, fourth or fifth work of grace, but an everlasting growth in grace and a constant advancement in the love of God and knowledge of our Lord Jesus Christ.

If the reader never felt the fire that comes with the Baptism of the Holy Ghost, let him never rest until he finds it. If he once had it and lost it, may he never stop unil he recovers the holy flame.

Happy the man who has it, happy the man who keeps it, and blessed is the man who knows how to spread it.

> "Refining FIRE go through my heart,
> Illuminate my soul,
> Scatter thy life through every part
> And SANCTIFY the whole."

CHAPTER XVIII.

THE GREAT REMEDY.

THE astonishing fact we are called upon continually to notice, is the ignorance of men concerning the omnipotence of grace in the Atonement: the almighty power of the Blood of Christ to save, recover, restore, renew, purify and uplift from the lowest depths to the greatest heights.

Christians who have felt the pardoning power, and believers who have experienced the sanctifying energy of the Blood certainly ought to realize what is meant by the redemption which is in Christ Jesus. And so some do have Christ-honoring views, and some have still nobler conceptions of the power of Jesus to save; but there are multitudes calling themselves Christians who do not seem to dream of the riches of grace in the Son of God, while the very strongest and most advanced still need to have their eyes opened with their faith limitation views, to see the wonders of salvation covered up in the words, "He is able to do exceeding abundantly for us above all we can ask or think"; and again, "If ye abide in me and my words abide in you, ye shall ask what ye will and it shall be done unto you." And still again two prayers for God's people, one in Colossians and the other in Ephesians, that seem to be horizonless, shoreless and bottomless, so far as grace is concerned in the human soul.

Most Christians have stationed the Blood at one or two points along the path of life. It is needed to get into the kingdom. Then it is needed to be made pure. Usually it is looked back upon, or forward to, as the man stands between pardon and holiness.

The thought of it rushing like a cleansing stream all along through life, ever powerful, and always in reach of the touch of faith, does not seem to enter many minds.

It is thought to be a periodic blessing, spasmodic rather than continuous. It is supposed to help in some cases, but not in all; when the great truth presented us in the Word is that the Blood is sufficient for all men, for all degrees of sin, for every kind of fall, and all the time. It is omnipotent saving grace perpetually applied.

There is no doubt in the mind of the author, that the church thus far has seen but little of the power of God in spiritual realms. We stand in awe over the sight of cyclones, tornadoes, floods and fires in Nature. Here is God's power in material things. But He has also omnipotence in the spiritual kingdom. It is not exercised by Him and beheld by us because we limit Him in that realm by unbelief. Nothing hinders God from working in Nature, but He can do nothing commensurate in the realm of spirit when unbelief reigns. The Gospel tells us that Christ did no mighty works in certain towns because of their unbelief.

So thus far we have seen God's love, God's mercy and God's wisdom, but God's power is to be beheld mainly in the future, perhaps not before the Millennium. We have fancied we have seen it already, but how little to what He can do, and will do, and that the human race will yet see and feel.

We have been accustomed to quote the scenes at the Day of Pentecost, and the great triumphs of apostolic times, as though the acme and climax of divine grace and power had been reached then; when we think there is no question but that which took place in those days was but a small sample of what is to be; a blossom from a garden, a sheaf waved in front of a vast coming harvest.

We marvel over meetings to-day where several hundred souls are saved, but where are the eyes of the reader not to see a time is prophesied as coming when a nation shall be born in a day! Christ will be seen riding at the head of the White Horse Calvary of Heaven, the work will be cut short in righteousness, and in the midst of the rush and tread and shock of armies in spiritual combat, a voice will be heard saying, "It is done—the kingdoms of this world have become the kingdoms of our Lord and His Christ."

The day of God's power will have come, and it comes because a full Gospel has been proclaimed. Men see the reach and perfect saving power of the Blood, faith springs up and God, who has long been waiting for that faith, and who can not work without it is exercised in Him, now arises to show what He can do.

And, oh, what will Christ not do, when every shackle and trammel and cord of man's unbelief that has bound Him is gone and He is free to save all, and to the uttermost round about the world!

How he has been belittled before men and made to appear as a helpless Saviour, when He was willing, able and ready to do exceeding abundantly for us all, the instant we came in faith unto Him.

Cities that rejected Him, towns which locked their gates, individuals who barred their hearts and lives against Him, and so created the idea of man's omnipotence and God's helplessness, will all go down together before Him in the latter day glory.

As the love of God and the grace of Christ are unfolded, and faith springs up, multitudes of the spiritually lame, sick, withered and impotent, the worst of sinners, the most hopeless of backsliders, chronic cases who have through many years been waiting for the moving of the water of life, will all rush forward, and nations will be born in a day.

What will be thought of in such times, of one hundred and twenty sanctified and three thousand converted, when a whole kingdom will turn to Christ between sunrise and sunset, and churches will be blazing with holy fire in every direction?

The cause of this stupendous victory will be seen to be in the acquired knowledge of the power of the Blood. When the completeness and perfectness of the antidote for sin is seen, the people will flock to the House of God like doves to the windows and be saved.

We are all familiar with the passage in which we are told that Christ is "made unto us wisdom and righteousness and sanctification and redemption." Concerning the first three we know something and yet far from all. As for the last word, "Redemption," the writer sees the gleam of unrisen suns, the glory of unborn days, and in a word, such tremendous possibilities and prophecies of grace through the atonement, that he would be afraid to disclose all that comes to his mind lest he be thought to be beside himself.

Redemption is a great word, and the work or works it stands for is vaster than many Christians imagine. Christ has come to destroy the works of the devil. He is to restore what Satan destroyed. He is to set up that which he cast down, and make right that which Satan made wrong.

He is to substitute order, harmony, melody, purity, happiness, life and salvation, for the discord, misrule, misery, sin and death set up by the Adversary. Just as we have seen a mother go through rooms that had been upset and disarranged by a set of mad-cap children, and quietly and patiently straighten and regulate from one end of the house to the other, until there was no sign of what the mischievous young ones had done; so is Christ to pass through the world and remove every trace of disorder, disturbance and confusion, all the evil and wrong, all the sin and sorrow introduced into it by the great common enemy of God and man, and make it look like a new world. He started the work two thousand years ago, and is still at it. He has already done much, but is to do more. It is the firm belief of the writer that when Christ completes His work this planet will look like Paradise restored. With sin, sorrow, sickness and death gone this world will no longer be called the devil's province or territory, but will fairly blaze and shine as it sweeps through the skies as the ante-chamber of Heaven.

With the knowledge of the power of the Blood, of what is in Redemption, the universal deliverance and perfect victory of salvation is certain to come.

Up to this time the great mass of Christians do not dream of the lengths, breadths, depths and heights in the plan of salvation for them. Few indeed are living the ever joyful, always victorious life that is our privilege through the grace and power of Christ. Perhaps no one, no matter how advanced in Christian experience, has seen and felt all that may be seen and felt, before the Lord's work is completed in us in this life.

The pity is that while God has placed an almighty recovering grace by the side of every man on earth in the Blood of His Son, yet men ignorant of the fact, or the measure of this salvation, go on in their sorrowful, staggering, faltering and even sinful way, until the end of life itself.

The Blood that is to save the world completely in the millennium, can save it now. The Blood that is to bring a nation to God in a day can bring the worst man to righteousness and keep him there safe and sound after he has been brought back.

It cleanseth from all sin. This is God's word, and no one can file exceptions after such an utterance without contradicting God. All sin means all sin.

And it cleanses now. It does not take time to cleanse. Time is no Saviour. There is nothing in the flight of hours and days to make the soul pure. The Blood alone can do this.

There is the strangest disposition upon the part of men to look elsewhere for cleansing and renewing rather than to the riven side of Christ. They exalt the flow of tears, the bitterness of their own repentance, the humiliation they entail on themselves, the promises they make, etc., etc., when not one of them can cleanse the soul.

These men have an idea that if they sin, it is wrong

and presumptuous to expect an instantaneous restoration. They think that a certain length of time spent in groaning, weeping and beating the breast will be very acceptable to God, and so after a while, after a sufficient time spent in doing penance, and humbling themselves before Him for the transgression, He for the sake of all these things as well as for Christ's sake will have mercy.

Great is the mistake. It does not take time to restore us. The Blood does it, and nothing but the Blood. Now if only the Blood can cleanse us from sin, where and how can we bring in Time as a factor of grace? The Blood cleanses from all sin, says the Bible, and it cleanses now.

As men take in the graciousness of these words, "all sin" and "now," it is going to work a revolution in the church and individual life. Thank God, it has already accomplished wonders with some, but this is the mere beginning.

It would certainly be surprising if God would originate a scheme of salvation that made no provision after the reception of pardon and holiness for possible lapses and falls. What an oversight it would have been on the part of divine wisdom, and in what terror God's people would be kept by the thought that if they transgressed from the way of holiness there was no method provided for bringing them back.

But God has made no such mistake. The Blood

which translates from the realms of darkness into the kingdom of light, and which makes us children of God and obtains the purification of the heart; that same Blood can recover if sin arises in the heart or the feet have gone astray. And it can do it effectually.

When an artillery wagon is constructed, we find that instead of four wheels, it is sent out into the field with five; the fifth wheel being tied on to the back axle tree, as a provision for the exigences and casualties of the battle. When a cannon ball sweeps away one of the four wheels the driver without a moment's hesitation leaps from his horse, cuts the fifth wheel loose, claps it on the axle, drops in the lynch-pin, springs into the saddle, pops his whip, and away he thunders with the rectified wagon.

As we note this piece of human foresight, we say will God have less? Will He send us out to front danger, where the shot and shell, the arrows and missiles of Satan are flying, where we may be struck painfully or mortally at any time, and yet have no plan of recovery for us? If this is so, then God has shown less thought and care in the plan of salvation, than the human workman did in the construction of an artillery wagon.

But He has not overlooked us. The Blood is the fifth wheel that will help us out of any and every spiritual difficulty. The instant we are shot by Satan, God's plan and provision for us is to fly to the Blood, have it instantly applied, be as immediately restored and go on our way rejoicing. All this was foreshadowed in the Trespass Offering, which, though of the same Blood as the Sin Offering, yet was a provision for the sins of ignorance, and we can easily see, for those transgressions that might come into the life of the believer, and which would not necessitate the same kind of approach as is seen in the first frightened and guilt-stained waiting upon God.

The Trespass Offering, while the same Blood, was an offering peculiarly for the child of God. The Israelite handled it, and not the alien and stranger.

This, of course, is not intended to teach that there is a necessity for sinning, but means that in case the servant of God should transgress he need not and should not despair.

The plain statement of the New Testament is that "The Blood of Jesus Christ His Son cleanseth us from all sin." This cleansing is in the present tense, and in a perpetual present tense.

The Blood, says the Bible, cleanses from *all* sin and cleanses from all sin *now*. Why, then, should we look to priests, pilgrimages, beads, prayers, tears and penances? Why indulge in hair-pullings, breast-beatings and bitter self-accusations? None of these things cleanse from sin. They do not cleanse now and never can purify. All of them have failed and will continue to fail. It is the Blood alone that cleanses from all sin. When will we get people to believe that blessed fact, and see them leaping, jumping and praising God through the temple?

If the heavy hearts, silent lips, drooping souls, troubled consciences and sin-defiled people all around us, could just get this wondrous truth into their minds and hearts, that the Blood cleanses from *all sin now*, they would be transformed in the flash of a moment into bright-faced, joyful-lipped, sunny-hearted Christians, whose very gladness would attract the multitude to Christ and whose lives would tell on the world for good not only for time but forever.

We have repeatedly said that if we were to sin, we would refuse to go into condemnation. And while bitterly regretting the occurrence, and repenting having been betrayed into the wrong thought, word or act, yet why allow hours and days of gloom to be spent in profitless repining and self-condemnation, that can never purify or restore.

Knowing that it is the Blood which cleanses we would throw everything on the altar, cry out to God: "O Lord, I am sorry that I sinned; I confess, renounce and repent the deed. But Jesus died and paid it all; all the debt I owe. I give up all to Thee. I put all on the altar. I look to Christ and believe what the Bible says, that the Blood of Christ cleanses from all sin now. I believe it, I believe it. Glory to God I believe it." And so I would continue to believe and plead with God, and lift up the Blood, and expect the fire until suddenly I felt the heart-warming soul-purifying touch, and heard the voice of the Spirit witnessing to the fact that all was well.

I would utter these words so frequently, so rapidly and so persistently that the devil himself would be confounded. He should have no opportunity of thrusting in an adverse and contradictory statement. I would repeat the words, holding them aloft as one would wave a banner, and stand on the Word looking up, believing and repeating, and repeating and believing until the fire fell and I could say again: "I feel the glory in my soul."

Naturalists tell of a small animal called the ichneumon which is not over two or three inches in size, but can defeat and destroy a venomous snake that is over a yard in length, and many times larger than itself. But it is noticeable that the ichneumon never fights over two or three feet away from a plant whose leaves contain the antidote for the snake bite. When the reptile plants its poisonous fangs in the little creature, the ichneumon at once drags itself to the bush, chews a leaf, is instantly restored, and returns refreshed and renewed to the conflict. After a little the ichneumon is bitten again, and feeling death creeping along the veins, flies at once to the shrub, takes another mouthful of the restoring leaf and returns with a new lease of strength and life to the battle. It is just a question of time. The snake grows weaker and weaker, while the ichneumon is continually renewed. So after awhile the larger animal goes down in the remarkable contest, and turning bottom side up, gives up the ghost, while the ichneumon, flushed, triumphant and jubilant, waves its right forepaw in the air (figuratively speaking), and almost shouts hallelujah.

So in the soul's great contest with Satan and sin, the disparity is great. Hopeless indeed would be the soul if left alone in the warfare against the great fallen Archangel who has led whole nations astray, and for six thousand years has become infernally wise in the ways of drawing men into transgression and perdition. But happily for us the tree of life with healing in the leaves grows close by each heart. The Blood of Christ, which purges the poison of hell from the soul, and makes the spirit clean white and beautiful, is flowing always in touch of the wounded heart. When smitten by Satan, and hurt through the imagination, desire, speech or action, we should instantly touch the blessed Christ who is always near, and that touch will instantly renew and restore. As many, says the Scripture, as touched Him were made perfectly whole. And so back to the fight we go; and if wounded again instantly look to Jesus and touch Him by another act of faith, and so keep on touching until perfect victory is won, the enemy driven from the field, and we are triumphant in the possession of the knowledge and ability how to resist Satan and conquer sin, and thrilled with the experience of constant cleansing, constant peace, and constant victory through Jesus Christ our Lord.

There are wearied and discouraged hearts all over the land, that ought not to be cast down, and would not be so if they could see the recovering, restoring power of the Blood.

Some have failed in the Christian life in various ways, and think now that there is not a single hope or prospect left. The grace of God has been abused, the talents entrusted them have been buried or squandered, and they can see nothing left but moral bankruptcy or life failure.

And so it would be if there was only one member to the spiritual firm. But we read that God is a co-worker in the matter of salvation. And He is the Great One of the life partnership. We may be upset, and the Lord remain unmoved.

Recently we read of a wealthy, benevolent gentleman who conceived quite an interest in a ragged urchin of New York. He found that the boy was anxious to do something to make a living, but lacked the small capital of a few dollars to begin and carry on the humble business as a bootblack. The gentleman purchased the necessary brushes and polishing material, and saw the boy commence business on a street corner with a radiant face. These two constituted the firm, the gentleman furnishing the material and the boy the hand-work. The lad did well, and by the third day had over a dollar in silver in his pockets over and above expenses. On the fourth morning, however, the gentleman missed the junior member of the firm from his corner, and later in the day saw him entering his office with a doleful countenance.

"Why, what is the matter?" he asked.

"It is all up. We are ruined!" replied the boy.

"What is up? Who is ruined? I don't understand you," said the gentleman.

"Oh," sighed the boy, "I mean you and I are done for—the firm's bursted!"

Little by little the senior member of the collapsed firm drew from the junior member his narration of distress. It seems that he the night before had attended some kind of Public Relief gathering where, under the influence of the songs, speeches and touching incidents related, the lad had responded to the appeal by emptying his pockets and donating his entire stock. Next morning as he felt his empty pockets, and surveyed his unoccupied street corner a revulsion of feeling and a sense of despair had settled down upon them. As he had expressed it, "The firm was bursted" and all hope was gone.

With great difficulty the gentleman concealed his amusement, and said to the junior member that while the break seemed to be very serious in his eyes, still it was not irremediable and he thought he could set him up and start him again. And so he did, to the great delight of the boy.

We of this earth are the junior members of the Great Firm of Salvation. As we falter, reel, and even break down here and there in the religious life, great is our gloom and despair. We say all is over; there is no more hope; the Firm is bursted.

Doubtless our despondency and gloomy speeches sound as absurd and are as amusing to angels and those who live in the Heavenly Courts as the boy's lamentation was to the millionaire. But they feel sorry for us in spite of their smiles, and would kindly stoop over us and say, "Not so, you are not ruined. The Blood is left; mercy and grace are left; and Christ is left. You may be undone, but He is not. Jesus Christ is the same yesterday, to-day and forever."

In a word, the junior member may be hurt, while the Senior Member is untouched and still has all power in heaven and in earth. He can set us up again, and cause us to resume business at the Old Stand, or further up Hallelujah Avenue in a more eligible situation, if necessary. Thank God for the renewing, recovering, restoring Blood of Christ.

We have found people strangely hindered and paralyzed with some sorrowful memory of the past. It was some disobedience to God, some failure in duty, perhaps some sin. Now, whenever they would arise

THE GREAT REMEDY.

and begin to do exploits for God, Satan brings back the remembrance and down they go in gloom, as they begin to doubt the power of the Blood to atone for and cover the past. They do not seem to realize that this very doubt is a limitation of salvation, a belittling of redemption, and another failure to see that the perfect remedy for all mistakes, failures and sins is in the Blood.

Surely if the Blood of Jesus can save a vile sinner, it can recover a wandering Christian. If it can cover a multitude of transgressions in the life of the unconverted, it can certainly atone for a few missteps or wrongs in the history of a child of God. Its virtue and power does not end in pardon, or even in holiness, but is for all people at all times and in all conditions.

We read in the old Testament that when God was preparing to bring His people out of Egypt on the night that the Death Angel was slaying the first born everywhere, He commanded that blood should be sprinkled on the door-posts and lintels of every house. His promise was:

"When I see the Blood I will pass over!"

What mercy and riches of grace are in this verse! What a world of comfort to every sin-sick heart and doubting soul!

Splash the Blood over your soul. Apply it by faith to the door-posts of your life. Sprinkle it on the past, present and future. Put it thick on every act of the past that you regret, but which you can not now undo. Thank God, we can do this. Now is it done? Is the Blood lifted up and relied on? Is it your only plea? If so, hear what God says and be glad forever, "When I see the Blood I will pass over."

What more can we ask for? And who can touch or harm one who is under the Blood? Pardon, purity, recovery, safety and Heaven are all in that Word.

In a great storm on our rocky coasts a ship was foundering. All the crew were soon swept into death save one sailor, who was seen clinging to the shrouds. The sea was so high that no boat could go to him. He was doomed, and he saw it as well as those on the shore. A trumpet was handed to a preacher to shout something to the man who would so soon be in Eternity. He took it in his hand with the mental question: "What shall I say?" Shall it be one of the points made in his sermon that Sunday morning? Meantime the man had only a few minutes to live. Under a happy inspiration the preacher, placing the trumpet to his mouth, cried out:

"Look to Jesus, man!"

The words were literally hurled through the stormy blast, and reached the exhausted sailor. In another moment came back the words:

"Aye, aye, sir."

And then they heard him singing; and they caught the words:

"Jesus, Lover of my soul,
　Let me to thy bosom fly,
While the nearer waters roll,
　While the tempest still is high."

He had reached the fifth line,

"Hide me, O my Saviour, hide,"

when they saw him loosen his hold on the wave-swept rigging and drop into the sea.

We have often thought of the scene, and feel to-day that if we had but one minute of time and one sentence to speak to each man on earth, that minute should be filled in every case with the sentence — "Look to Jesus."

It is the only thing we can do, and it is the best thing we can do, whether we be sinners, backsliders or faithful servants of God.

If we look to Jesus we will be saved; and if we continue looking to Jesus we will run patiently the race set before us, and will finally sit down with Christ on the right hand of the majesty on high.

Thank God for the Great Remedy, the cleansing keeping Blood, the omnipotence of grace in Jesus Christ. Let no one despair with such a complete and all-powerful salvation encompassing the life and springing up in the heart. No matter what may be the sin, Christ can forgive it; nor how great the mistake, He can overrule it; nor how dark the night, He can bring us out of it; nor how disastrous the defeat, He can make victory perch again upon the trailing banner. He is a mighty Saviour. His name is Jesus, and He has come to save His people, and He is doing it. We read that He is doing so, we see it, and above all we feel it. With such a Redeemer, whose compassions fail not, and whose power is infinite, we should all press on with glad hearts, being fully persuaded that He is able to keep that which we have committed unto Him, and will present us faultless at last before the Throne with exceeding joy. Amen and Amen.

THE END.

DR. CARRADINE'S LATEST BOOK,

The Sanctified Life

PRICE, $1.00

TABLE OF CONTENTS.

Different Theories in Regard to Sanctification.
The True Theory.
Obtainable Now.
May be Lost.
Can be Recovered.
How to Keep It
Some Features of the Sanctified Life.
Loneliness of the Life.
Prayer and Reading.

TABLE OF CONTENTS.

Witnessing.
Good Works.
Fasting,—Tithes—And Dress.
Moods, Affinities, and Impressions.
Doubts—Fears—Frets.
Come-Out-Ism — Put-Out-Ism.
Secret Societies.
Side Tracks.
The Great Remedy.

It shows people how to recover sanctification if lost, and how to keep it and never lose it. It illuminates, assists, strengthens, and settles and confirms them in the sanctified life.

THE BETTER WAY, = = 75 cts.

CONTENTS: 1. Opening Words. 2. The Better Redemption. 3. The Better Prayer. 4. The Better Hope. 5. The More Excellent Sacrifice. 6. The Better Covenant. 7. A Better Experience. 8. A Better Supping. 9. The More Excellent Way. 10. A Better Life. 11. A Deeper Salvation. 12. A Greater Privilege. 13. The Better Resurrection. 14. The Abundant Entrance into Heaven. 15. The Better Reward at the Judgment. 16. The Better Company in Heaven. 17. The Higher Grade in Eternity. 18. How to Enter. 19. Paul's Way. 20. The Saviour's Way. 21. The Methodist Way. 22. Witnesses in Wesley's Days. 23. Witnesses in Our Time. 24. How I Entered In.

The Ram's Horn: "A BIBLE GALLERY of BEAUTIFUL PICTURES of the better way."

Northern Christian Advocate: "His style is fresh and vigorous, and spirit most commendable."

The Author: "I think this book will be more convincing and effective in bringing people into the blessing of sanctification than any other book I have written."

Post-paid, 75c. Agents wanted. Write for special rates by the quantity.

Other Books by Bro. Carradine.—Sanctification, 80c ; The Second Blessing in Symbol, $1.00 ; A Journey to Palestine, $1.50 ; The Bottle, 25c ; Twenty Objections to Church Entertainments, 50c.; The Old Man, $1.00 ; Pastoral Sketches, $1.00 ; Sermons, $1.00.

ORDER OF THIS OFFICE.

A PENTECOSTAL LIBRARY. . . .

BY S. A. KEEN, | The Pentecostal Pastor Evangelist.

PENTECOSTAL PAPERS.

CONTENTS:

The Pentecostal Promise.
The Pentecostal Gift.
The Pentecostal Fulness.
The Pentecostal Baptism.
The Pentecostal Anointing.
The Pentecostal Bestowment.

FIFTY CENTS.

Faith Papers. | Teaching when, what, and how to believe, and results of believing. 40c.

Praise Papers. | Dr. Keen's spiritual autobiography, with portrait and closing chapter by his wife on his Pentecostal translation. 30c.

Salvation Papers. | Dr. Keen's last book. Nine lucid chapters on "Personal," "Present," "Future," and "Perfect" Salvation. 35c.

From the Niagara of commendatory notices, we clip the following

INTERDENOMINATIONAL INDORSEMENT.

Methodist Mention: "I wish a million copies might be sold and read."—*Bishop Mallalieu.*

United Brethren Testimony: "It is a book for all, especially for those who earnestly desire and honestly seek the blessing of full salvation."—*Religious Telescope.*

Presbyterian Praise: "Without question, his words and influence have been powerful for the promotion of high and happy Christian life."—*Herald and Presbyter.*

Baptist Indorsement: "Incident and illustration are freely used in making plain God's teachings."—*Christian Observer.*

OVER EIGHTY THOUSAND ISSUED.

NOW READY.

GODBEY'S NEW TESTAMENT COMMENTARY.

Volume II.
- Hebrews—Perfection
- James—Practice.
- Peter—Fire.
- John—Love.
- Jude—Lightning.

NOTICE.

1. It is condensed. It omits all passages which need no explaining, and deals thoroughly with the difficult ones, thus giving the reader the greatest possible value for his money.

2. It throws floods of new light upon many important passages.

3. It shows the proper translation of the New Testament, and sweeps sophistical arguments against holiness triumphantly from the field.

4. It will doubtless be the great Holiness Commentary on the New Testament for coming years, as it is written from a holiness standpoint by one of the ablest evangelistic Greek New Testament translators of any age.

434 pages.   PRICE, $1.25, post-paid.

The Fourth Edition of Volume I., "REVELATION"--$1.00

IS ALREADY ISSUED.

The General Verdict of its readers is voiced in the following, taken from like notices:

Of intense interest.—*The Methodist.*

Practical, spiritual, interesting and instructive.—*Religious Telescope.*

The clearest exposition of that "mysterious" book that we have yet seen.—*Gospel Banner.*

I am sure there is not its like in all the literature on Revelation.—*Presiding Elder H. O. Moore.*

A REMARKABLE BOOK, ... worth much to thoughtful people.—*T. H. B. Anderson, in Methodist editorial.*

A GRAPHIC AND POWERFUL representation of the author's interpretation.—*Michigan Christian Advocate.*

It is by a VIGOROUS thinker and PUNGENT writer. It is worthy a thoughtful and prayerful perusal.—*Guide to Holiness.*

Twenty per cent. discount to all who order of us the whole set. Three volumes more to be published. Each volume to be paid for yearly as issued.

Agents Wanted.   Address

Full - Salvation - Library

BY ...
MARTIN WELLS KNAPP.

OVER SEVENTY THOUSAND ISSUED!

The following are among the terms used by readers to express their appreciation of them:

* * *

APT,
ABLE,
ATTRACTIVE,
ORIGINAL,
STARTLING,
EVANGELICAL.

* * *

* * *

TERSE,
GLOWING,
VIGOROUS,
FASCINATING,
THRILLING,
DELIGHTFUL.

* * *

Out of Egypt into Canaan, Or, Lessons in Spiritual Geography, shows how to escape the bondage of sin, and gain the liberty of the Canaan experience of entire sanctification. **80c.**
"Able, clear, and forcible."—*Central Methodist.*

Christ Crowned Within. This book shows the gracious privilege and result of coronation of Christ within the believer's heart. **75c.**
"A treasury of the burning thoughts of those who have lived nearest the Master."—*Bishop McCabe.*

Revival Kindlings Is full of choice Revival facts and incidents collected from the best sources. **$1.**
"It will be read with comfort and delight."—*Mich. Christian Advocate.*

Revival Tornadoes. Life of Rev. J. H. Weber, Evangelist. This book describes the Revivals of this successful Evangelist, and points to the secrets of soul-winning success. **$1.**
"A keen exposure of sham Revivals."—*Christian Standard.*

"Impressions" Helps to detect the nature of impressions, and shows whether they are from above or below. **50c.**
"A most instructive, suggestive, and useful book."—*S. A. Keen.*
"We advise everybody to read it."—*Central Baptist.*

The Double Cure Sets the truth of entire sanctification in clear, Scriptural light, and answers objections to it. One of the best of the author's books. **25c.**

The above books have been warmly indorsed by the religious press; but above that, God has wonderfully used them to lead many to Christ, and establish multitudes in the experiences of salvation.

They should be in every home and Sunday-school. Sent postpaid on receipt of price.

HOLDING OUT...

By E. P. ELLYSON, | A MINISTER OF THE FRIENDS CHURCH.

It is written especially for YOUNG CONVERTS, and for NEW ARRIVALS in the LAND OF CANAAN, and is . . well adapted to that end. . .

It is sweet, clear, true, warm, and evangelical. It is not only a safe, but an effective book to help lead and establish in the experiences of . . Salvation. . .

CONTENTS:

Chapter I—Keep Consecrated. Chapter II—Keep Believing. Chapter III—Keep Telling It. Chapter IV—Keep Telling It, Cont. Chapter V—Keep Denying. Chapter VI—Keep Watching. Chapter VII—Keep Faithful to the Spirit's Leading. Chapter VIII—Keep Using the Means of Grace. Chapter IX—Keep Using the Means of Grace, Cont. Chapter X—Keep Humble and Courageous. Chapter XI—Keep Busy. Chapter XII—Keeping Busy and Its Temptations. Chapter XIII—Live by the Moment.

Price, Cloth, 35 cents.

"IMPRESSIONS"

PRICE, **FROM ABOVE,** 50c.

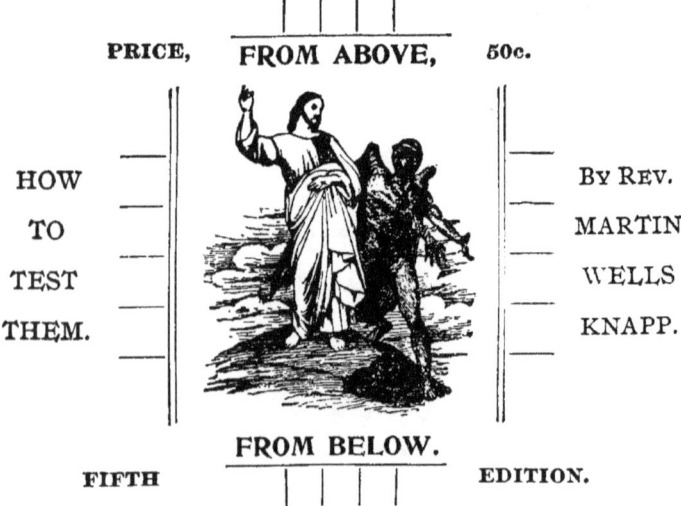

HOW TO TEST THEM.

By Rev. MARTIN WELLS KNAPP.

FROM BELOW.

FIFTH EDITION.

CONTENTS: I. Impressions: Their Origin. II and III. Impressions from Below. IV. Results of Following Them. V. How to Test Them. VI. Practical Application of Preceding Principles. VII. Impressions from Above—Divine Guidance Guaranteed. VIII. Conditions of being Led by Them. IX. Convictions from Above—Results of Following Them. X. The Christian's Perfect Model.

WHAT THEY SAY ABOUT IT.

Many witness to being wonderfully helped by this book. Its indorsement is voiced in the following from many like notices:

Get It. It ought to be read by all Christians. Get it for your Sunday-school library.—*Methodist Herald.*

Worthy. Ought to be circulated widely.—*Christian Witness.*

For Everybody. We advise everybody to read it.—*Central Baptist, St. Louis.*

An Admirable Safeguard on the subject of Spirit guidance.—*Evangelist S. A. Keen.*

Alive. A live book on a very important subject.—*Christian Standard.*

Helpful. A helpful volume. Much to correct wrong inferences.—*Baptist Herald, Detroit.*

Gospel Gem. The book is a Gospel gem, and its perusal will greatly benefit all who anxiously desire to escape the snares of the devil, and seek to be led by the Spirit of God.—*Religious Telescope, Dayton, O.*

A Corrective. It will help to correct some foolish notions entertained by some not well instructed people, manifest in crazy utterances and wild-fire demonstrations, such as bring the doctrine of Holiness into disrepute.—*Rev. J. C. Floyd in Northwestern Christian Advocate.*

Practical. This is a volume embracing religious truth of a practical nature.—*Religious Herald.*

Enthusiastic. The author is enthusiastic in the presentation of his subject. His book will do good wherever read.—*Western Christian Advocate.*

Tears and Triumphs
~No. 2.~
By L. L. PICKETT and M. W. KNAPP.

One of the Best Song Books for the Price Ever Issued.

It is Pentecostal, Evangelical, Loyal.

It is printed in round and shaped notes, contains a Topical Index, an Index of Choruses, and single songs worth more than its price.

It contains the merits intensified which pushed the sale of "Tears and Triumphs" No. 1 in so short a time to

. . **OVER 100,000 COPIES** . .

One firm ordered 2,000 before the book appeared. Others are buying by the hundred and thousand. From the

NIAGARA OF PRAISE

which it is receiving the following few drops have been selected:

Western Christian Advocate, Cincinnati.—"Will be greatly appreciated by lovers of inspiring song in Sunday-school and revival work."

Rev. J. C. Johnson.—"I had four dozen yesterday and sold them in a few minutes. Its soul-stirring songs take with all denominations."

A Teacher and Composer orders 200 and writes: "I do not hesitate to pronounce it one of the best books for the purpose intended now on the market; a marvel of completeness."

Evangelist D. B. Gernigan.—"We sold the last one of the song books, 150, before the meeting closed. It is a book for the people. They shout and cry as they sing. It is the best book I ever saw."

Mrs. O. C. McGarvey, Music Teacher.—"It is better adapted to revival meetings than any book we have ever seen. I consider it a collection of the most spiritual songs I have ever seen."

G. E. Kersey, Teacher and Musical Composer.—"It is the best new song book on the market for camp-meeting, revival, church and home."

W. M. Patty.—"Indeed, it is a triumph in the interest of holy song."

⁎⁎ *It is adapted to Evangelistic Work, Camp-Meetings, Prayer and Praise Meetings, Sunday-schools and General Church Worship.*

Such men as Hoffman, Bryant, Sweney, Palmer, Ogden, Kirkpatrick, Kieffer, McIntosh, Tillman, Lincoln, Street, Black, T. E. Perkins, W. O. Perkins, Rev. J. E. Rankin, Gilmour and many others have assisted in making it.

☞ Try the following: Nos. 5, 6, 7, 32, 35, 38, 58, 60, 62, 63, 70, 76, 85, 91, 94, 116, 118, 121, 125, 132, 133, 147, 149, 154, 155, 163, 168, 179, 180, 187, 193, 195, 196, 199. If not pleased, return it and get your money back.

PRICES: Board, 25c. prepaid; $2.80 per doz. prepaid; $20 per 100 not prepaid. Muslin, 20c. prepaid; $2.25 per doz. prepaid; $16 per 100 not prepaid. Printed in round and shaped notes. State which you wish.

ORDER OF THIS OFFICE.

Holiness and Power,

By Rev. A. M. HILLS,

Minister and Evangelist in the Congregational Church.

Able . . Original **Forceful Convincing**

IT TREATS:

The Disease.—The Remedy.—How to Obtain the Blessing.—Results of Obtaining It.

Every lesser issue is left out and the main theme, **Holiness and Power,** is experimentally, Scripturally, luminously and mightily magnified. The following are a few of many

WITNESSES TO ITS WORTH:

N. Y. Christian Advocate.—"It is a strong, forceful, earnest presentation of great truths, too often misunderstood and neglected."

Western Christian Advocate.—"Mr. Hills is eminently Christian in spirit, and deals with the great subject earnestly and forcefully."

St. Louis Christian Advocate.—"As a historical reference book on the subject it has marked values."

Religious Telescope.—"Those desiring additional light on this subject will do well to procure and read this book."

Way of Faith.—"One of the best treatises we have seen on the subject of experimental and practical holiness. The author has forged his book on the anvil of Scripture statement, confirmed it by his own clear blessed experience."

A Correspondent writes:—"I sent a copy to a student, a beautiful young man. In just a week it guided him into the experience of entire sanctification."

Over 386 large pages from new type, neatly printed and bound. **Price, $1.15.**

Special discounts, as usual, by the quantity, and to ministers.

AGENTS WANTED.

IMPORTANT ANNOUNCEMENT.

A NEW ENTERPRISE.

PENTECOSTAL HOLINESS LIBRARY FOR 1898.

Less than a Dime a Copy by the Year.

IN addition to the Full Salvation Quarterly, which is not published frequently enough to meet the need of such a publication, we have decided to publish a **Pentecostal Library** on Salvation subjects, each monthly issue, like that of the Quarterly, to be complete in itself. Its object is:

FIRST. TO SPREAD THE TRUTH AND COUNTERACT THE INFLUENCE OF ERRONEOUS LITERATURE ON PENTECOSTAL LINES WHICH IS BEING SO WIDELY CIRCULATED.

SECOND. TO FURNISH SUCH READING AT A LOW PRICE.

We are enabled to do this through the sacrifice of authors in furnishing us their writings and through donating much valuable time and taking the risk of financial loss, which we we are willing to do for the truth's sake.

We feel God has been leading us toward taking this step for some time, but have recently come to our final decision.

The following is part of the bill of fare which is being prepared. Full announcement will be made later.

LOOKOUT FOR SOME DELIGHTFUL SURPRISES.

We expect to begin the year with

Pentecostal Wine from Bible Grapes, Year Book for 1898, by Carradine, Rees, Godbey, Ruth, Pickett and others.

We design also publishing a number of sections of **Lightning Bolts,** our new book, as issues of this Library. Also,

Kept by the Spirit; or, Trials and Triumphs, by Amanda Smith.

Popery to Pentecost, by J. S. Dempster, a converted Romanist.

Choice Stories for the Young.

Types of the Holy Spirit, by an eminent author, and other productions which we believe will be the very

CREAM OF PENTECOSTAL HOLINESS LITERATURE

of the present time. Possibly we may reprint some expensive books which God has wonderfully used, thus bringing their price within reach of all.

If you favor this movement to help flood the land with **pure Holiness** literature at low prices, and will remit for the year on receipt of the **January number,** please drop me a card to that effect immediately, as we wish to have as large a list of advance subscribers as possible to enter the Library at the Postoffice Department.

Price per year, 12 numbers, $1.00.

It and the Quarterly or Revivalist, $1.25.   .   .   All three, $1.50.

May I not hear from you in regard to it by return mail? Address

The Full Salvation Quarterly for 1898.

FOUR HOLINESS BOOKLETS
Postpaid, for Only 30 Cents.

January.—"Salvation Melodies." Abridged from Tears and Triumphs, Nos. 1 and 2.
April.—"Gibeonites No. 2; or, Helps to Holiness," by B. S. Taylor.
July.—See Later Notice.
October.—See Later Notice.

CHOICE, CHEAP, CONDENSED. 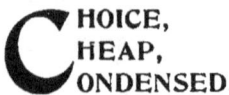  **SAFE, SOUND, SATISFYING.**

NOW IS THE TIME TO SUBSCRIBE.

30c. Per Year. It and the Pentecostal Holiness Library, $1.25. The Revivalist and both, $1.50.

CHEAPER THAN NOVELS.

Novels Inflame, Dwarf and Ruin.
These Stimulate, Delight and Edify.

The following **back numbers** can be had on receipt of price:

1895.
1. The Double Cure, M. W. Knapp.
2. Spiritual Gifts and Graces, W. B. Godbey.
3. Victory, W. B. Godbey.
4. Holy Land, W. B. Godbey.

1896.
5. Salvation Papers, S. A. Keen.
6. The Better Way (abridged), B. Carradine.
7. (Out of Print.)
8. Sins versus Infirmities, B. S. Taylor.

1897.
9. Pentecostal Sanctification, S. A. Keen.
10. The Ideal Pentecostal Church, Seth C. Rees.
11. Pentecostal Preachers, M. W. Knapp.
12. The Sanctified Life (abridged), B. Carradine.

10c. Each, *Special Rates by the Quantity.*

If you believe in first-class Holiness literature at low prices; if you desire to help spread Scriptural Holiness; if you want booklets so condensed that you can get time to read them, and yet so readable that they will not tire, then get the above.
Over 50,000 copies proves The Quarterly's worth.
May we not hear from you? Address

www.ingramcontent.com/pod-product-compliance
Lightning Source LLC
Chambersburg PA
CBHW051748040426
42446CB00007B/275